HX. LADIES' COLLEGE.
Pleasant St.

GORDON & KEITH,
Manufacturers of Furniture and
Dealer in House Furnishings.
Halifax, N. S., and Sydney, C. B.

McALPINE PUB. CO., Ltd.
Printers, Lithographers, etc.
Sackville, Cor. Granville. Phone 16.

A. O'CONNOR & CO.
Millinery, Children's Dresses
and Underwear,
47 and 49 Barrington St.

"THE HERALD,"
Morning Herald & Evening Mail.
Cor. Granville and George Sts

PICKFORD & BLACK,
Steamships,
81 Upper Water St.

SIMSON BROS. & CO.,
Wholesale Druggists,
Ordnance Square.

A. M. BELL & CO.
Wholesale and Retail Hardware,
67 and 69 Upper Water St.

MOIR, SON & CO.
Bakers and Confectioners,
Cor. Argyle and Duke Sts.

FARQUHAR BROS.
Gasfitters, Tinsmiths & Plumbers,
Cor. Blower and Barrington Sts.

CHRONICLE PUB. CO.
Chronicle and Echo,
10 and 12 Prince St.

N. S. NURSERY,
Plants, Cut Flowers, Bouquets
and Floral Designs,
Opposite Railway Station.

McAlpine Map of Halifax, 1900

A Victorian Lady's Album
Kate Shannon's Halifax and Boston Diary of 1892

Della Stanley

A Carolyn MacGregor Book

Formac Publishing Company Limited
Halifax and Boston 1994

The development and pre-publication work on this project was funded in part by the Canada/Nova Scotia Cooperation Agreement on Cultural Development. Formac Publishing Company Limited acknowledges the support of the Canada Council and the Nova Scotia Department of Tourism and Culture in the development of writing and publishing in Canada.

Canadian Cataloguing in Publication Data

Stanley, Della Margaret Maude, 1950-

Main entry under title
  A Victorian Lady's Album: Kate Shannon's Halifax and Boston Diary of 1892

ISBN 0-88780-231-1

1. Shannon, Kate Winnifred — Diaries. 2. Young women — Nova Scotia —Halifax — Diaries. 3. Halifax (N.S.) — Biography. I. Stanley, Della Margaret Maude. II. Title.

FC2346.26.S42A3 1993 971.6'22503'092 C93-098671-7 F1039.5.H17S42 1993

Formac Publishing Company Limited
5502 Atlantic Street
Halifax, Nova Scotia B3H 1G4

Printed and bound in Canada

Distributed in the United States by:
Formac Distributing Limited
121 Mount Vernon Street,
Boston, Mass 02108

Visuals credits

The publishers wish to acknowledge with thanks the assistance and co-operation of the archivists and staff at the Public Archives of Nova Scotia (PANS), whose collections form the basis of the visual material reproduced here. Thanks are due also to the librarians and archivists at Special Collections, Killam Library, Dalhousie University; the Maritime Museum, Halifax; the Bangor Public Library; and the Boston Athenaeum.

The period visual material used in this book is drawn from the following sources: Kate Shannon's diary is held by the Public Archives of Nova Scotia (PANS, MG1 Vol 802 F/2) and is reproduced with permission. The diary contains Kate's occasional pen-and-ink drawings and sketches. Extracts from the diary itself are reproduced on many pages, including her self-portrait (page 60) and several other small drawings. The photographs, paintings, newspaper and magazine extracts and advertisements are largely drawn from the PANS photography, manuscript and map collections. Extensive use was made of the editorial content and the ads published in 1892 in the pages of the *Acadian Recorder*, Halifax. The Kenny scrapbook in the manuscripts collection, PANS, is the source of several visiting cards, menus and other print items reproduced here. The Bangor Public Library provided the issues of *Popular Science News* that carried contributions written by Kate Shannon. Illustrations from Christmas, New Year's and visiting cards are drawn from the private collection of Margaret Black. The coloured postcards are from the private collection of Doris Hilchey.

The cover reproduces a detail from a painting by F. M. Jones Bannerman, PANS; also the girl at the piano (page 27)is taken from a Bannerman painting, PANS. The wild flower illustrations are by A. L. Pratt, PANS.

Other visual credits: end paper map, map collection, PANS; p.i, C. M. Bowman, PANS; p.5, Cogswell collection, PANS; p.7, Notman collection, PANS; p.11, Thornvale (the Kenny home), Mrs. Kenny's dance card, Kenny scrapbook, PANS; p.13, Notman collection, PANS; p.17, PANS; p.21, p.23, Kate Shannon's diary; p.27, F. M. Jones Bannerman, PANS: p.31, PANS; p.37, PANS; p.39, Annie Bruce, PANS; p.43, Shannon family; p.47, *S.S. Halifax*, Maritime Museum; p.51, PANS; p.55, p.59, Boston Athenaeum; p.60, Kate Shannon's diary; p.61, Boston Athenaeum; p.63, Special Collections, Killam Library, Dalhousie University; p.65, Copley Square, Boston Athenaeum; p.67, *S.S. Halifax*, Maritime Museum; p.75, PANS; p.77, Armstrong-Archibald collection, PANS; p.79, Notman collection, PANS; p.85, Notman collection, PANS; p.93, West Hants Historical Society Collection, PANS; p.97, Cogswell collection, PANS; p.99, Maplewood, Royal Engineers Collection, PANS; p.103, Notman collection, PANS; p.109, St. Margaret's Bay Historical Society collection, PANS; p.108, Chief Justice James McDonald; p.111, Special Collections, Killam Library, Dalhousie University; p.113, Doris Hilchey; p.115, Cogswell collection, PANS; p.119, Kate Shannon's diary. Photography of paintings: Gary Castle.

Preface

In 1985, I was asked to prepare a biography of the Hon. Judge Samuel Leonard Shannon for the Dictionary of Canadian Biography. While conducting my research, I came across a collection of the Judge's papers at the Provincial Archives of Nova Scotia. Among those papers was a small, very worn diary dated 1892 and inscribed with the name of its young author, Kate Winnifred Shannon. I soon found myself straying from the writings and papers of Judge Shannon. The diary of his then eighteen-year-old daughter was both fascinating and haunting. I wanted to read the whole diary and was anxious to find out what had transpired during the year in which it was written. I discovered the private confessional of an adolescent girl caught between the old, status quo world of her aging parents and the modern, changing world of her contemporaries.

Following her premature death from tuberculosis at the age of twenty-one, Kate Shannon's diary had been carefully and lovingly preserved by family members among the private papers of her father, who had himself died only a few months before his youngest daughter. While Judge Shannon's papers are valuable sources of information about the legal and political aspects of the life of a leading public figure in nineteenth-century Halifax, Kate's seemingly insignificant diary provides a wealth of information of another kind. It reveals much about family and community life from the unique perspective of a young woman: how time and space were ordered; how family and community expectations were realized; and how social, religious and cultural values were expressed in an upper-middle class, urban, professional, Christian, Anglo-Saxon Maritime household. It is the record of life in the traditional "domestic sphere" of late Victorian women. The immediacy of the detail is striking. Reading this journal one witnesses, virtually first hand, the daily habits and social values of a private woman. Above all, the diary portrays what life was like for a girl on the verge of adulthood. "It is such a very sudden and odd change to have my hair up and long skirts that it gives me the very remarkable feeling as if I were playing charades all the time," Kate writes.

Kate Shannon's diary is not the typical diary of a young person who might simply record the weather or inconsequential day-to-day data. Certainly, such elements are present; but there is more. Here one also finds an account of personal inner conflict and self-analysis. As Kate says of herself, "The trouble is that I am eccentric.... I sometimes think that I won't live very long, or else end my days in an insane asylum." This diary is the story of the dreams and despairs of a young woman who wanted far more out of life than her health and home environment allowed. It is the work of a person who possessed a degree of literary talent which enabled her to pen an interesting, informative and readable diary. For this reason, and because I found myself referring students of Canadian social and women's history to it on a number of occasions, I became convinced that Kate Shannon's diary was of both historical and general importance, particularly for those interested in Victoriana, in the history of Halifax and in women's history.

In editing the diary, my first priority was to preserve the integrity of the original format. However, to prevent awkward interruptions and confusion for the reader, full names and phrases were inserted where initials and short forms had been used. For instance, Kate usually identified family members and close friends with the initial of their first name; her favorite short form was N.P.H. for "Nothing particular happened." Where spellings varied, such as "stayed" and "staid," the more modern was adopted throughout. Errors in grammar were corrected only for the purposes of clarification.

Victorian ladies were particularly fond of preserving the precious bits and pieces of their lives and age in the form of scrapbooks and albums. Technological advances in photography and colour reproduction provided them with seemingly endless sources of material — from pressed wildflowers to newspapers clippings, from brightly coloured stickers of birds and roses to elaborate cards bearing sweet sentiments, from detailed Notman photographs to softly tinted postcards of home and far away exotic places. In order to present Kate's diary in the form of a Victorian album, illustrative materials were drawn from many sources, both public and private. Some of Kate's own pen-and-ink sketches from the original diary have been reproduced. The ever popular postcards of the late 1890s and early 1900s provided wonderful colour views of Halifax and Boston. Local newspapers like the *Acadian Recorder*, period books and magazines such as *The Child's Companion* and *St. Nicholas*, painting collections and carefully preserved scrapbooks were rich sources for late nineteenth-century Victoriana. Photographs of people and places mentioned by Kate came primarily from the Public Archives of Nova Scotia and the decendants of Judge Shannon.

A number of people have assisted me in bringing this diary of a young Victorian lady out of the obscurity of the Archives. First, I must thank all those at the Public Archives of Nova Scotia who put up with my constant questioning and requests for assistance — in particular, Allan Dunlop, Margaret Campbell, Lois Yorke and Darlene Brine. Among those helpful others who assisted me in tracking down illustrations and valuable clues were Karen Smith of Special Collections and Charles Armour of the Dalhousie University Archives, both at the Killam Library, Dalhousie University; Marvin Moore and Mary Blackford at the Maritime Museum of the Atlantic; Eric Ruff, Laura Bradley and Capt. Hubert Hall of the Yarmouth County Museum; Cindy Todd of the Bangor Public Library; and Catharina Slautterback of the Library of the Boston Athenaeum. To Doris Hilchey, who supplied her mother's fabulous collection of postcards, to Margaret Black, who provided a wonderful collection of Victorian cards and stickers, and to my mother, Ruth Stanley, who never fails to be a source of information, I offer very special thanks.

Without the careful typing by Sheila McSeveney the text might very well still be in its original form. To Kevin O'Reilly and Todd Hawkins, the designers who have done a wonderful job of capturing the flavour of Kate's diary and her time, and to Shawn Connors, the patient production miracle worker, my congratulations. Finally, without the interest and enthusiasm of Carolyn MacGregor and the guiding hand of Jim Lorimer, this diary would most certainly never have been published.

I want to thank each and every one of the members of the Shannon family who tried so hard to locate photographs and to clarify the family tree: Anne F. Carswell, Mary Anne Carswell, Errol Mitchell, Helen Shannon, Isabel Morrow, Len Tweddie, Richard C. Shannon, Robert S. Shannon and Ethelyn Marshall. I enjoyed and appreciated every piece of correspondence.

For help in more than one way, but especially for their patience and encouragement, I thank my two Thomases.

Finally, I must thank Miss Kate Winnifred Shannon. I wish I had known her.

I dedicate the final product to my six-year-old son, Thomas Edward George Stanley Cromwell, who has just completed his first school journal.

Introduction

"She was of a sunny, cheerful disposition, gentle, even tempered, patient and self denying." So wrote James Shannon of his youngest sister. Yet, Kate Winnifred Shannon left to posterity a somewhat less romantic self portrait. From the pages of her diary, written in her eighteenth year, emerges a young girl bursting to explore worlds beyond the confines of her home. She was prevented from doing so by physical limitations, family expectations and social customs.

Kate was loving and loyal; she had a great sense of fun and humour. But she was also lonely, bored, frustrated and confused. As her great niece observed upon reading the journal, "I noticed how circumscribed and narrowing her life experiences were. That she was not permitted higher education. That she had few friends.... She was held particularly close by her family, not permitted to have much of a life.... What more she could have made of her life had she been given the chance. No wonder she had the blues! Yet, her intelligence and spirit shine so clearly from the pages."

Upon entering the confessional world of this talented and intelligent diarist, the modern reader becomes more of a participant than an observer. One moves in with a family that experiences its share of squabbles and teasing, tension and love. Interestingly enough, some family relationships were little different from those of similar families today. One observes, of course, a very traditional home where things are generally quiet and sedate. One reads of the household duties, the illnesses and the celebrations. One meets family friends, the majority of whom were from well known legal, political and business families of Halifax like the Payzants,

Oxleys, Jones, McInnis, Grahams, Motts, Geldarts, Twinings, Sedgewicks, Macdonalds and Tuppers.

The Shannon household in 1892 was relatively typical of its social status and era. Judge Samuel Leonard Shannon, Kate's father, was the dignified head of the family. At age 76, he was a highly respected figure in Halifax society. Not surprisingly, imperial sentiments and intellectual interests were part and parcel of Shannon's home. His grandfather was a New Hampshire Loyalist, and Shannon retained a strong sense of loyalty to the British Crown and held British values throughout his life. His father had been a successful dry goods merchant in Halifax and his mother was the sister of Charles Allison, founder of the Mount Allison Boys' Academy and Ladies' College, the forerunners of Mount Allison University. While studying at King's College in Windsor, Nova Scotia, Shannon developed a life-long fascination with history and classics. However, he chose the law as his profession and began to practise in 1839 in Halifax, where he quickly developed a reputation for his methodical manner, high moral standards and skills as a solicitor.

In his spare time Judge Shannon was an avid reader and community worker. Over the years he had been commissioned with the Second Halifax Militia, was a volunteer fireman, and had served on the Nova Scotia Railway Board, the Dalhousie Board of Governors, the Young Men's Christian Association and the British and Foreign Bible Society. He was also one of the founders of the Dalhousie Law School and taught at that institution for several years. In 1847, he undertook a nine-month tour of Europe and Great Britain, which provided him with material for years of public speaking. Combining his oratorical skills and his public concern, Shannon became a Member of the Provincial Legislature and was a Minister in the government of Charles Tupper. He supported the completion of the Intercolonial Railway, Confederation and free common schools. In 1881 he was appointed a Judge of Probate.

Never robust, Shannon's health began to deteriorate in the mid-1880s and by 1892 he was virtually blind, and very frail. However he continued to be a lively storyteller and keen reader. Young Kate regularly read to her father and accompanied him on his walks to the courthouse, barber shop and the nearby Public Gardens. It was perhaps on these walks that Kate first acquired her love of botany, since her father had always been interested in horticulture and had been an enthusiastic supporter of the original plans to develop the Public Gardens.

Shannon's home was quiet in spite of the presence of five children between the ages of thirteen and twenty-seven. Ever courteous, refined and urbane, Shannon set high ideals for himself and those around him. He expected his Methodist, Tory home to epitomize the values of sobriety, morality, patience, hard work, thrift and piety. Religious faith was important to the Shannon household, and regular attendance at Grafton Street Methodist Church and participation in church-related activities dominated Sundays.

Although the Shannons had a maid and washing was sent out, the Judge's wife, Annie Fellowes, nineteen years his junior, really ran the household and cared for the family. She found additional fulfilment in her charitable and benevolent work with the Grafton Street Methodist Church, the Sailors' Home, and the Women's Christian Temperance Union. While the W.C.T.U. fostered

women's causes and social concerns, Annie Shannon and her daughters clearly were not avid suffragettes or equality-minded feminists. Rather, they were of the maternal feminist school of social crusaders who perceived the domestic and public roles of women to be guardian of the family and social virtue, respectively. None of Annie's daughters appear to have joined in their mother's activities which, at the time, were the most common means by which middle-class women sought personal identity, intellectual stimulation and limited social independence in a society marked by male decision-making and legal and social double standards. There is nothing to suggest that either Kate or her sisters were encouraged to join their contemporaries, either, who were breaking the educational, legal, medical, scientific, political and business barriers of a paternalistic public world. Interestingly enough her father had supported the decision to grant women entrance into Dalhousie College on the same conditions as male students, but it would appear that none of the Shannon women chose to pursue a university education.

Kate, in particular, was treated like a delicate plant requiring protection. She lived according to the ideal of Victorian womanhood, which "combined religious piety, moral purity and — first and foremost — a complete commitment to domesticity" (J.White, *Sisters and Solidarity*, p.3). Kate was not afraid, however, to express her views of the male sex: "Men will come first when and how it suits themselves no matter who else may be put out," she writes.

The Shannons lived in a large, but not ostentatious, three-storey brick and stone house at the corner of Spring Garden Road and Brenton Street. They were just a block from the Public Gardens and within easy walking distance of the Court House, the Drill Shed, the Sacred Heart Convent, Saint Mary's Cathedral and several grocery and dry goods stores, all of which were on Spring Garden Road. While it was not regarded as one of the trendy upper-middle class areas, neighbours did include Daniel Cronan (one of the wealthiest dry goods merchants in the city), two lawyers, John Payzant and William Twining, and several other leading businessmen, such as Charles Anderson and Adam Burns. The house included seven bedrooms, a large formal drawing-room, a dining-room, kitchen, and study as well a several smaller rooms and a basement. It was heated by hot water, lit by gas, and indoor plumbing was installed in 1892 as noted in Kate's diary. Furnished according to Victorian taste, dark oak, walnut and mahogany furniture rested on rich Brussels carpets. As well, there were two grand pianos, numerous shelves and cupboards for books and knicknacks, mirrors, needlework and the inevitable moose head.

The Shannon family, c. 1879-1880. Left to right: Elizabeth Grafton (Bessie); Samuel Leonard (Len); Mrs. Shannon holding Francis Sutherland (Frank); Mary Josephine (Josie); Kate Winnifred (Kate); James Noble (Jim); Judge Shannon. In front, Edward Grafton (Ted). Missing is Minetta Ballister (Nettie).

Such were the comforts for those children still living at home: "Ted," or Edward Grafton, was a teller with the Halifax Banking Co., and was courting "Maggie" (Margaret A. Bill), his future wife; "Bessie," or Elizabeth Grafton and "Josie," or Mary Josephine — both in their mid-twenties — were unmarried; Kate; and her thirteen-year-old brother "Frank," or Francis Sutherland. A regular visitor was the eldest daughter "Nettie," or Minetta Ballister, who had recently married Wallace Macdonald, the son of the Chief Justice of Nova Scotia. Wallace was practising law in Halifax with his brother James. He and Minetta had a son in April 1893. The eldest son "Jim," or James Noble, also a lawyer, lived in Toronto with his wife "Lilly," or Elizabeth Shaw, and their daughter Lillie Marion. The remaining son, "Len," or Samuel Leonard, was an accountant in Berwick, Nova Scotia, where he lived with his wife "Bert," or Beatrice M. Bacon, and their daughter "Bee," or Beatrice. A second daughter, Mary Leonard, was born in 1892.

Through the daily diary entries the reader comes to know Kate Shannon in all of her strengths and weaknesses. One meets her closest friends, Millie Cady and Winnie Burns, and aches with her as she tries to understand why a "wedge" threatens to change those friendships forever. One sympathizes with her over the indignities of medical visits and monthly periods, the frustrations of wearing long dresses and the tedium of a "routine much the same every day." One is with her on her long and often lonely walks, and in her moments of deepest depression, despair, self-evaluation and self-questioning. One rejoices with her in Boston as she matures and blossoms with the excitement and stimulation of new places to see, things to do and people to meet. One grows with her as she acquires the trappings of womanhood. Like any well-attired lady of the 1890s, Kate dressed in tailored suits, tight-fitted jackets, gored skirts, high-collared blouses, tafetta petticoats, and buttoned boots; she pulled her hair up over a "rat" to acquire the dignified silhouette of the fashionable ladies in *Harper's Bazaar* and the *Ladies' Journal*.

The reader also comes to appreciate Kate's special forms of refuge: walking in the Public Gardens, in Point Pleasant Park and through the estate lands of Oaklands and Maplewood on the Northwest Arm; reading romantic epic poetry by people such as Longfellow, and moralistic and romantic novels such as *Lady Jane* and *Davey and the Goblin* (which first appeared in serial form in two of her favourite magazines, *St. Nicholas* and *Harper's Young People*, respectively); playing her favourite games, including the board game "Halma" and the guessing game "Up Jenkins"; and of course, writing in her diary. Perhaps most important of all, the reader comes to realize how much Kate is starved for intellectual stimulation. Lessons in German and French offer her no satisfaction, probably because there is little practical use for them in her life. Occasionally, she read some more serious literature such as *Pilgrim's Progress*, *Walden: or Life in the Woods* and *The Last Days of Pompeii* but she makes little comment about their content. Although, like most young Victorian women, she appreciates art and music, she derives limited pleasure from either. She dislikes to practise and tackles sewing and needlework solely for practical purposes. It is clear that Kate

Shannon wants something more out of life than what she is experiencing.

Kate's only truly fulfilling interest is the study of natural science, particularly botany, about which she is quite knowledgeable. Collecting and classifying botanical specimens whets her natural curiosity. The gifts of a microscope and a copy of a botanical text by the famous American botanist Asa Gray are much treasured, and she is very particular about her purchase of a vasculum in which she collects and preserves her freshly discovered specimens. As the corresponding member for the Halifax Chapter of the Agassiz Association, named for the eminent Swiss-American naturalist, Louis Agassiz (whom she virtually worships), Kate periodically prepares illustrated reports on local plants for the Boston-based magazine *Popular Science News*. This allows her to combine her artistic and literary skills and to reach out to the world beyond 58 Spring Garden Road.

Perhaps like most eighteen-year-olds Kate's interests are with her family, friends, domestic activities and botany, not in weighty social, economic and political concerns of the public arena. Nevertheless, the insularity of Kate's domestic perspective leaves the reader with little impression of the national, let alone international, context of 1892. There is not a word about German militarization, American industrialization or French imperialism. Nothing is said of English preparations for Queen Victoria's Silver Jubilee four years hence. There is no sense that the death in June 1891 of the Conservative Prime Minister Sir John A. Macdonald had thrown about five million Canadians into a state of political turmoil; that his reluctant successor, J. J. C. Abbott, in November 1892, turned the leadership over to the Halifax lawyer, John S. D. Thompson, who was confronted with the task of pulling together his party and his

country at a time when conflict frustrated many aspects of national life — French versus English, Catholic versus Protestant, provincial interests versus federal, imperialist versus nationalist versus continentalist, free trader versus protectionist, Anglo-Saxon versus non-Anglo-Saxon. Nothing is said of political concerns such as the Manitoba Schools issue, provincial autonomy, immigration policy and western development, the introduction of the first Criminal Code or rising anti-Oriental sentiment in the West.

Economic conditions do not concern Kate either. There is no mention that Canadians in 1892 were just beginning to see signs that the worst of the worldwide depression that had taken hold in the late 1880s might be over. There is no comment on the social dislocation and injustices that plagued a rapidly industrializing and urbanizing Canada — poverty, unemployment, alcoholism, labour unrest, prostitution, drug abuse, juvenile crime, family disintegration, racism. There is no hint of the dramatic social changes that were taking place in the areas of education, women's rights and emancipation, child welfare and factory legislation. Although Kate records her first ride on an elevator and an electric tram, nothing is said of other scientific, mechanical and technological developments of the age which were revolutionizing the way Canadians lived and worked: the theories of germ propagation and human evolution; the telephone and telegraph; the washing machine, the typewriter; half-tone newspaper photos. Only indirectly does the diary allude to the new craze of bicycling that was sweeping the country, the emergence of tourism as a growth industry, the proliferation of "ready made" consumer goods including clothes, cleaning products and food, and the Victorian fascination with natural history and horticulture which resulted in the fashionable diversion of sci-

entist and dilettante alike to collect everything from shells to butterflies, and to plant elaborate public and private flowerbeds laid out in geometrical designs.

Although she took little interest in the political and economic world around her, Kate Shannon, following her month in Boston, came to realize just how provincial and insular Halifax really was: "I get so ashamed of Halifax with its dirty sidewalks, disreputable Museum and forlorn Library to say nothing of other causes of disgust." Kate probably knew little of the "dark side" of Halifax, the drunks, criminals, prostitutes and destitute. She probably had little or no contact with the minority peoples such as the Blacks or the Micmac. But she did recognize Halifax's failings and would have argued with a contemporary, W.H. Howard, who wrote, "Halifax is a beautiful city from whatever point of view the observation is taken,...this fair and flourishing city by the sea."

In fact, although most upper- and middle-class Haligonians would not have realized it, Halifax was in the final years of imperial prosperity and gentility. Ten years later its social and economic decline would be obvious. This city of over 40,000 people, which had just celebrated its 140th birthday, was living through the last years of garrison life. The military and naval presence that had shaped so many of the social standards and activities as well as the business and employment opportunities of the past would be gone by 1906-7. But in 1892, military parades, band concerts, receptions, parties, polo games and fancy dress balls still dictated the social calendars of young eligible women and their parents.

Halifax was more than a military town; there were political, professional, business and academic communities, all of which influenced the tastes and activities of the social elite. It was because of this ecclectic social mix that Halifax was able to boast a fairly respectable array of cultural activities. There were regular military band concerts in the Public Gardens, music hall and play productions in the Lyceum and Orpheus Theatres, learned lectures on religion, philosophy, history and science at Dalhousie College and various churches, and concerts given by the students and teachers at the Academy of Music. Depending upon the season there were also celebratory parades such as the one for Labour Day, fireworks after regattas on the Northwest Arm, skating at the Exhibition Building, sailing at the Royal Nova Scotia Yacht Squadron and a seemingly endless array of At Homes. But, whatever the event, Victorian respectability, propriety and godliness officially prevailed.

Halifax of 1892 revelled in the burst of economic growth that marked the early 1890s. New buildings sprang up to accommodate the increasing population and expansion in the areas of education services and municipal government. The Forrest Building at Dalhousie College had been completed in 1888 and the new City Hall and School for the Blind in 1891. An explosion in residential housing saw the opening of lands around the College, Richmond, Merkelsfield, Quinpool Road and Mumford Road areas. As well, the city officers were working to upgrade once disreputable streets including Barrack and Water.

Like the rest of Canada, Halifax was being shaped by urban growth, social change, the women's movement and technological advances. Haligonians may have complained of high property taxes, but they also boasted of their modern services, the wonders of electric street lights, the increasing number of telephones, the introduction of electric trams, and a new dry dock to repair large vessels like the British flagship, *Blake*. Supplying the garrison was still a major factor in the economy of the city. However, in recent years, a diversity of commercial and manufacturing businesses had emerged producing sugar, shoes, cotton, pianos, rope, soap, brushes, skates, paint, tobacco, biscuits, candles, spices and railway supplies. Goods were shipped to and from Great Britain, the West Indies, New England and central Canada. With the completion of the Intercolonial Railway, Halifax dreamed of becoming the principal year-round shipping port for Canada.

In the end, these dreams were not to be realized. Montreal and New York supplanted Halifax as a shipping port. Immigration programmes funnelled new arrivals away to the West. Central Canadian expansion attracted Maritime workers away from home, and Halifax investors and business people were slow to counter the resultant economic decline. However, in 1892, few were concerned. Things looked very good for those who lived in what was then one of the wealthiest cities in Canada.

This was Kate Shannon's Halifax: comfortable if a bit shabby; a city with many beautiful vantage points; where the mail was delivered twice a day; where British imperial sympathies were openly expressed; where money was tastefully and quietly spent; where family and commercial ties with New England were still strong; where Lieutenant Governor Malachy B. Daly and General Sir John Ross, Commander of the British Forces in Canada, presided over the social calendar; where a Liberal Premier, W. S. Fielding, sought to improve his province's financial position within the Canadian federation; where merchants and wholesalers dominated the economic scene; and where Kate Winnifred Shannon celebrated her eighteenth year.

Della Stanley
August 1993

Related Reading

ALLEN, R. *The Social Passion: Religion and Social Reform in Canada, 1914-28.* Toronto, 1973.

Bacchi, C. L. *Liberation Deferred? The Ideas of the English-Canadian Suffragists, 1877-1918.* Toronto, 1983.

Backhouse, C. *Petticoats and Prejudice: Woman and Law in Nineteenth-Century Canada.* Toronto, 1991.

Blakeley, P. R. *Glimpses of Halifax from 1867-1900.* Halifax (PANS), 1949.

Beck, J.M. *Politics of Nova Scotia: Nicholson - Fielding, 1710-1896,* Vol. I. Tantallon, N. S., 1985.

Berger, C. *Science, God and Nature in Victorian Canada.* Toronto, 1983.

Callwood, J. *The Naughty Nineties, 1890-1900.* Toronto, 1971.

Conrad, C., et al. *No Place Like Home: Diaries and Letters of Nova Scotia Women, 1771-1938.* Halifax, 1988.

Fingard, J. *Jack in Port: Sailortowns of Eastern Canada.* Toronto, 1982.

Fingard, J. *The Dark Side of Life in Victorian Halifax.* Halifax, 1989.

Granatstein, J. L., et al. Nation: *Canada Since Confederation,* 3rd ed. Toronto, 1990.

Hodgson, G. E. *Shannon Geneology.* Rochester, 1905.

Howard, W. H. *Glimpses In and About Halifax.* Halifax, 1896.

L'Esperance, J. *The Widening Sphere: Women in Canada, 1878-1940.* Ottawa, 1982.

McCann, L. "The 1890s: Fragmentation and the New Social Order" in *The Atlantic Provinces in Confederation,* E. R. Forbes and D. A. Muise, ed. Toronto, 1993: 119-154.

Newman, P. C. *Canada 1892: Portrait of a Promised Land.* Toronto, 1992.

Payzant, J. M. *Halifax: Cornerstone of Canada.* Burlington, 1985.

Peck, M. B. *A Nova Scotia Album: Glimpses of the Way We Were.* Willowdale, 1989.

Peck, M. B. *A Full House and Fine Singing: Diaries and Letters of Sadie Harper Allen.* Fredericton, 1992.

Prentice, A., et al. *The History of Canadian Women.* Toronto, 1988.

Raddall, T. H. *Halifax: Warden of the North.* Toronto, reprinted 1971.

Regan, J. W. *Sketches and Traditions of the Northwest Arm.* Halifax, 1908.

Stanley, D. M. M. "Samuel Leonard Shannon: The First Downtowner." *Hearsay* (Spring 1986): 21.

Stong-Boag, V. and Fellman, A., ed. *Rethinking Canada: The Promise of Women's History.* Toronto, 1986.

Waite, P. B. *Canada, 1874-1896: Arduous Destiny.* Toronto, 1971.

White J. *Sisters & Solidarity: Women and Unions in Canada.* Toronto, 1993.

January

Fri. 1st. Here I am started in a new diary. I don't think I will write so finely in this book and perhaps I may put in a few feelings to flavour my bare record of facts and to aid me in putting my thoughts into suitable language. I wonder whether anything very shocking, terrible, or sad will have to be chronicled in these pages? I sincerely hope and pray to the contrary, but whatever happens it is a great comfort to know that God is ruling everything for the best. However, this is going a good way beyond my usual meagre outline of events. Nothing very particular happened today; in the afternoon Mother, Bessie and Josie received visitors — only eleven honouring them — and I went with Millie over to see Winnie. She had afternoon tea, as she often has, and before that we had some games of Geography. (Weather cold frozen dull bleak and threatening snow.)

Sat. 2nd. Had Millie, Winnie, Lidy and Una Gray to tea. They came quite late, nearly 6 o'clock it was in fact before they all arrived but Millie and Winnie had been out skating. I asked Lucy Cady to come too but she had a cold which was too bad for her to come. We five with Bessie and Josie had tea early before the others. Frank went out to Nettie's for the night. After tea there was a book from the Bolster boys for me; it was called "Confessions" and I got pen and ink and all the girls wrote in it. It just came at a nice time. My botany book came too, and it is lovely. We played Literature, a spelling game, Hunt the Thimble and had refreshments, nuts, raisins and oranges. They all left about 9:30 and I *think* they had a good time. (Cold, frozen, fair.)

Sun. 3rd. Rainy, so didn't go out. Frank didn't come in.

Mon. 4th. It was rainy all day and so dark I could hardly see to do anything. Frank came home early morning. Evening *tried* to think up an Agassiz Association report. (As I said, rainy all day.)[1]

Tue. 5th. Afternoon Millie and I went over to Winnie's and assisted in the rite of doughnut frying. (Mild, fair.) Got more things from the Bolsters; I got another little silk handkerchief, this one is plain white, hemstitched. This makes the third silk handkerchief.

Wed. 6th. Morning made an appointment with Dr. Delaney. (Fine, till evening when it snowed, hailed and then rained.)

Thurs. 7th. Afternoon Millie and I went over to Winnie's. (Morning terribly rainy and windy; afternoon not bad.)

Fri. 8th. Morning in town with Millie. Afternoon short walk with Millie and Winnie. (Beautifully fine.) Wrote to Mrs. Bolster evening.

Sat. 9th. Nettie came in to dinner. Millie and I went in town afternoon; she got photos of herself, Lidy, Winnie, and Mary which they had had taken and kept secret from me. They are very good; and they each gave me one. (Beautifully fine and mild.)

Mon. 11th. Had quite a day of it, for at half-past 9 I went to be tortured at Dr. Delaney's, and when I was through with him Bessie met me and we went in to

Dr. Dodge's, to have him examine my eyes. He made me read printed letters from quite a distance, and look at the gas through some queer looking tin kind of instrument, and finally dropped atrophine into one of my eyes. When we were through with him we hunted all over the town to find some paper suitable for the covers of my "Popular Science News" which I am binding, but without success. Then about 3 o'clock we two started off for Dr. Dodge's again thereby missing seeing Nettie for any length of time, as she came in just as we were getting off and was gone before we were back. This time he made me read the letters again and then gave me a prescription for atrophine drops to be put in my eye twice a day, which (when I got home) I posted off to Buckley's to get made up, having to wait half an hour, more or less, for it. Then in the evening Ted and Josie went to meet Edith Rand but missed her and she got here first. She came to stay the night and leave the next day for Sackville; this was better for her than to wait five hours for her train at Windsor Junction, which she would have been obliged to do if she hadn't come here. (Dull, rather cold and frozen.)

Tue. 12th. Had lunch at 1 p.m. and then Josie and I went with Edith to see her off at the station. When we had got home Millie came up and we went over to Winnie's. Lidy was gone back to school. Bessie went out to Nettie's for day and night. (Like yesterday very much.) Got letter from "Little Mabel" — a case of mental telegraphy; saw "Harper's Monthly" for December.[2]

Wed. 13th. Morning to the dentist and oculist's. Bessie came home afternoon. (Morning dull and afternoon rainy.)

Thurs. 14th. Morning got "mental telegraphy" note from H.H. Ballard. Afternoon Millie and I were over at Winnie's. Prince Edward, Duke of Clarence, died today, and also Cardinal Manning whoever he might be. (Dull, foggy, drizzly, and sometimes very rainy, mild, close.)[3]

Fri. 15th. In house all day. Millie came up afternoon. (Dull, foggy and rainy. *When* will it be fine!) I think "mental telegraphy" is all a fraud, didn't get a letter I wrote to myself and Josie was likewise disappointed!

Sat. 16th. Afternoon in town with Millie. (Actually cold, and frozen, though mostly dull and bleak.)

Sun. 17th. Church morning. Afternoon went with Bessie to see ruins of Salvation Army building burnt last night. (Glorious cold frozen fine winter day.)

Mon. 18th. Sarah here. Millie came up afternoon and we played Tic Tac Toe and Information. (Snow and rainy.)

Tue. 19th. Sarah here. Finished "Popular Science News" which I have bound. (Mild and very rainy. Turned cold and snowed night.)

Wed. 20th. Ted came home from the bank with chills and fever and went to bed. I went afternoon for the sake of the walk to take some papers to Mrs. Twining. This is the day of the Prince's funeral and they fired minute guns and tolled bells in the afternoon. There is snow on the ground and I actually saw *two* sleighs! though all the other vehicles were on wheels. (Cold, very snowy at times.)

Thurs. 21st. Ted came home early yesterday and went

Mr. Kenny.

Lady Sinclair
at Home

Wednesday June 26th 4-7.

25. Onslow Square.

to bed ill with chills and fever and today is still in bed though better. Afternoon went with Millie and Winnie to see if Collin's Hill is good for coasting, but they've put a fence right in the way! A beautifully fine winter's day with the exception of there being no sleighing, but the snow hurt my eyes so I could hardly open them all the while I was out.

Fri. 22nd. Morning went into town when Bessie went in with Father, and after we had left him we went to get a "gem" taken of Bessie, and then we finally went to Dr. Dodge's where he tested left eye and gave me a prescription for a pair of glasses, so then we trotted off and bought the glasses and created a small excitement in the family circle by my appearance in them. Nettie was in and stayed till after lunch. Afternoon went by myself to the Library; Millie and Winnie being at the rink — the first day they have been able to go owing to want of ice! Ted better but still in bed. (Magnificently fine day — snow not gone yet!)

Sat. 23rd. Astonished Millie when she came up this morning by my glassy visage. She brought Winnie over to see and admire also. Afternoon about 6, Frank and I went into town to buy a "Progress." (Morning rainy and snowy; afternoon snowy, cleared rather and growing colder.)[4]

Sun. 24th. Nettie and Wallace came in to dinner. Morning went to church, wore glasses. (Beautifully fine but very cold and frozen, snow still on ground, icy.)

Mon. 25th. Sarah here. Stayed in and sewed. (Snowy all day, moderating.)!!!!!!!!!!!!

Tue. 26th. About 12:30 p.m. Andrew's sleigh came for us and Mother, Josie, Sarah (who was here today) and I all went out to Nettie's where we had lunch and came back about 2:30 leaving Josie there to stay with Nettie. Sarah had a good look all over the place, not having been out there before. Nettie was ill having had a bad attack of something which, if not "Grip," was certainly very much like it. (Fair, mild and melting.) Ted being recovered went back to the bank today.[5]

Wed. 27th. Afternoon went to with Mother to see Frank coasting on City Hill and then to see old Mrs. Freeman. Didn't want to go there but couldn't desert Mother. Josie came afternoon. Went to Winnie's to return books; she, Millie, and Mary had been tobogganing. (Morning rather mild; frozen though with some snow on the ground, growing colder, afternoon very fine.)

Thurs. 28th. Afternoon escorted Mother to the Sailors' Home, and then went to the Library. (Milder, somewhat, very fine.)

Fri. 29th. Afternoon went with Mother to the W.C.T.U. [Women's Christian Temperance Union]; came home and stayed in the rest. (Like yesterday).

Sat. 30th. Millie and Winnie came in for a few minutes morning. Afternoon finished "Lessons in Botany." (Raw cold day.)

Sun. 31st. Church morning. Hymns afternoon. (Morning fairly fine, finally sleety, more snow from the N.E.)

went by myself to the Library; M. & W. being at the rink — The first day they have been able to go owing to want of ice! — Ted better but still in bed. (Magnificiently fine day - snow not gone yet!)

February

Mon. 1st. Afternoon to the Library. Nothing particular happened besides. (Perfectly glorious winter day, splendid sleighing, a glistening crust on the snow and a slight silver thaw on the trees which was lovely in the sun.) Got letters from Mrs. Bolster — one for me.

Tue. 2nd. Afternoon Bessie and I went for a walk down towards the Park; we did not mean to go far at all, but we finally drifted all the way around the Point! One can hardly imagine a more perfect winter's day and we enjoyed it to the full; it was so good to be in the dear woods again and everything looked most charming, the effect of sun on sea and snow and snow-strewn trees being indescribable, to my poor pen anyway. There wasn't very much to botanize but I brought home a "winter bouquet" all the same. (Very fine, mild, though the crust on the snow was very hard and frozen.)

Wed. 3rd. Afternoon tobogganing with Millie and Winnie, Lalia Graham was with us. Lovely time. (Dull, with cool wind.)

Thurs. 4th. Afternoon about 5 went to fetch Mother home from W.C.T.U., then ran over to see Winnie. (Snowy, very windy and quite blizzardy though not very cold.)

Fri. 5th. Afternoon for a walk, went to Miss Allison's for papers for Mother. (Dull, sprinkling snow very cold and N. wind.)

Sat. 6th. Morning in town by myself; afternoon with Millie over to Nettie's; not to tea though. (Cold with high cold wind.) Lucy Macdonald was here to dinner.

Mon. 8th. Afternoon Millie and I went over to Winnie's for awhile. (All the morning a hard snow storm; afternoon cleared finally.)

Tue. 9th. Nettie came in about 10 o'clock and stayed till half-past 12 when she went in to the dentist's. She came back when she was finished bringing Lucy Macdonald whom she met in town with her, and stayed till about 5. She drove in and out both, for the snow is thick and heavy. I went in with her when she went to town, escorted her down to Dr. Merrill's door, and then went down to Margeson's; got two photos of Bessie. Then went to the Library and was rowed by old Creed. Evening wrote to Edith, got a letter from her morning. (Charming winter day, lots of snow, rather mild.) [6]

Wed. 10th. Nettie came in afternoon, stayed to dinner. She paid one or two calls and went to the Payzants' 5 o'clock tea with Bessie and walked home about 7:30, taking Ted out to stay with her as Wallace had to go off electioneering. (Glorious fine bright day; rather mild.) Went for a little walk with Bessie after she came home; I had about half a dozen bad tempers before I went out but the walk made me feel a little better dispositioned.

Thurs. 11th. Ted came home sick from Nettie's afternoon, and had the doctor. Election day. (Very high wind dull, threatening rain; sleighing still good.) [7]

Fri. 12th. Afternoon Josie and I escorted Mother to the W.C.T.U. and then we went down to see the Great Travelling Hat and Bear, which are to be shown at the World's Fair (when they get there). Ted better but still in bed. Stairs and Kenny re-elected yesterday, hooray.

STREET SCENE IN WINTER. HALIFAX, N.S.

One can hardly imagine a more perfect winter's day & we enjoyed it to the full; it was so good to be in the dear woods again and everything looked most charming, the effect of sun on sea and snow & snow-strewn trees being indescribable, to my poor pen anyway. There wasn't very much to eat but I brought home a winter bouquet all the same. (Very fine mild through the crust)

(Tremendous snow and wind storm last night, snow drifted from Dan to Beer-sheba. I think it must have rained after that. Anyway it was pretty slushy today. Mild dull nasty.)[8]

Sat. 13th. Morning Millie and Winnie dropped in to see me after being in town. Afternoon Millie came up and we went over to Winnie's and then we all went tobogganing and had a fine time. Then we played "Information" for a while over at Winnie's. (Rather dull and windy, cold and frozen.)

Sun. 14th. Church morning, afternoon read aloud to Josie who had a very bad cold. (Fine cold and frozen.)

Mon. 15th. Afternoon Millie and I were over at Winnie's and we had the kitchen to ourselves and did fancy cooking! (Rainy foggy dismal day.)

Tue. 16th. Morning went for the doctor. Mother got the Grip, badly. Afternoon to the Library. (Colder, *very* slippery.)

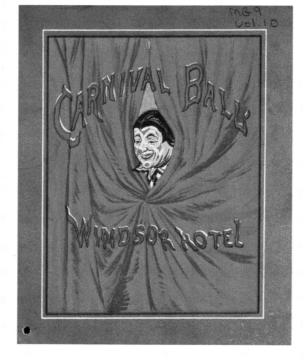

Wed. 17th. Mother better. Afternoon was with Millie and Winnie. Wrote to Jen. (Fine, very cold, icy.)

Thurs., Fri., Sat., Sun., Mon., Tue., and Wed. 24th were a good deal alike and very unpleasant. On Thursday I took ill with a horrid heavy cold and went to bed in the afternoon. Friday p.m. I was up all day but felt very badly at night so stayed in bed all Saturday morning till after dinner. Meanwhile, Father was taken ill which upset things all round generally, and by the time I was getting up Frank had to go to bed with Grip. On Sunday only Bessie went to church morning. Only Josie to Sunday School and Ted and Josie in the evening. Today (Thursday) we are all much better and the Dr. has paid his last visit today. Millie and Winnie have neglected me for fear of getting Grip, but they sent me yesterday a huge envelope with poetry in it, so this afternoon I wrote them an answer. (Flurries of snow, raw.) During the week the sleighing has entirely disappeared, partly from rain and partly from the sun. By Monday or Tuesday I think the sleighing was spoilt, but the dirty banks of snow remain in place to testify to the depth of snow we had.

Fri. 26th. Afternoon walked down with Mother to W.C.T.U. Winnie came over to see me. (Fine and rather mild.)

Sat. 27th. Morning Millie came to see me and Millie and I were there afternoon. Josie has a horrid cold today. (Fine, *very* cold.) Blanche and Mr. Wesendonge were in here this morning. They arrived last night.

Mon. 29th. Blanche and Mr. Wesendonge were in here afternoon. Josie has had Grip we think. (I think cold and disagreeable; I was not out anyway.)

PROGRAMME 1885 ENGAGEMENTS

Bonjour
Estudiantina
Wanderlust
Moonlit
Casino
Maid of Kent
Mother Hubbard
La Venitienne
Liederkranz
Mariana

1. Lady Baird
2. Fecht about the Fireside
Sweet Smiles
Lyra
West Side
Laguna
Evelyn
Recite d'Amour

Au Revoir

1. Lancers
2. Waltz
3. Galop
4. Waltz
5. Lancers
6. Waltz
7. Polka
8. Waltz
9. Lancers
10. Waltz
11. Scotch Reel
12. Waltz
13. Polka
14. Lancers
15. Waltz
16. Polka
17. Waltz
18. Waltz
19. Waltz
20.

Sir Roger de Coverly

Section.

1.
2.
3.
4.
5.
6.
7.
8.
9.
10.
11.
12.
13.
14.
15.
16.
17.
18.
19.
20.

March

Tue. 1st. How glad I am that we have got on as far as March! It came in in quite a lamb-like manner, not stormy that is, but it wasn't a very pleasant day, dull, with a raw cold wind. I walked with Mother as far as Grafton Street as she was going to a meeting in the church and was not sorry to come right home. —— I hope we will have an early spring.

Wed. 2nd. I cannot say that this day has been one of unalloyed bliss, by reason of some wretched "maltine and cod liver oil" which Josie and I began to take today, horrid stuff! The day seemed cold, raw and disagreeable so I did not venture out but finished "Rudder Grange" to Josie and also did some reading on my own account. Millie and Winnie dropped in to see me on their way to the rink. Evening brooded over an Agassiz Association report; not fun!

Thurs. 3rd. Poor Father is having a long siege of it. He does not get up till late in the morning, and then goes to bed again very early. He has not been able to come down stairs once yet; he has grown very weak and looks awfully pulled down. However, he seems to be getting better so we hope it may not be long before he is himself again. What did I do today? Not very much. Took that nasty dose three times and lacked gratitude for it. Read a little, and tried hard to get started on my report but didn't succeed in this endeavour till evening when I did get ahead a little, though 'twill all have to be boiled down and cooked over. (Snowed, hailed, and rained. Snow deep, walking awful, sleighs out.)

Fri. 4th. Read, and thought, and had some awfully crazy feelings. The trouble is I am eccentric. Even Langford McCoy seems to have noticed it for he asked Frank if that sister (meaning me) wasn't a little queer. I believe Frank replied that I was a little off, or something of the kind, so I suppose I may look forward to being known some time as "the Miss Shannon that's a little out, you know, — the one with the glasses." Josie says I might wear a placard with "Eccentric but Harmless" printed on it. I sometimes think that I won't live very long, or else end my days in an insane asylum. I hope that isn't wicked to think, and I suppose I have no business to be so morbid, but I don't seem able to help it somehow and isn't it enough to make one dismal to have to take that maltine and cod liver oil three times? Well anyway with two of us taking it three times a day it ought not to last long. —— Thought over my report which, luckily, doesn't have to go till Monday. (Weather rainy, dreary looking day, slush deep and snow very dirty.)

Sat. 5th. Morning Nettie came in; we have not seen her for a long while, for we couldn't get out to see her, and Wallace had the Grip and she had it again herself. I went in town with her and then she came here to dinner and stayed till about 4 p.m. Wallace came to meet her and they both drove home in a sleigh. After they had gone Millie and Winnie came over to see me. Evening Josie read "Rudder Grange" to Ted. (Dull, somewhat mild, walking awful.)

Sun. 6th. Snowed all day. Didn't go out.

Mon. 7th. Afternoon Nettie came and stayed till half-past 5. Bessie and I went in town, paid Dr. Dodge a final visit to report how my glasses work, and I inquired for vasculums at Cragg's and was told they could make me one. (Dull, inclined to rain.)[9]

Tue. 8th. Dr. Read came in afternoon to see how we were all getting along. Winnie came in while he was upstairs and got nicely caught. She heard him coming downstairs and scuttled around Bessie's chair to hide but she was too big, she couldn't find a place and had to stand up to see him. He greeted her characteristically. "Is this Winnie? Little Winnie no longer!" Poor Win! her face was a sight to see. In the morning I forgot to say Josie and I went for a walk out to the Willow Tree and back Jubilee Road. The walking was execrable. But the event of the day took place when we were all cosily settled in the dining room after dinner. The door opened and an old man came in (I don't know if he *is* old or not but he certainly looked so then) though neither Josie, Frank, or I knew who it was. Bessie fortunately recognized him and cried "Why, *Uncle John* !" *Then* we knew who it was! He's come to stay, we don't know how long! (Perfect day except for the walking, too fine to last and proved a weather-breeder.)

Wed. 9th. Well, I got my report off today anyway. I am not at all satisfied with it but I couldn't write it all out again for the third time, to say nothing of ten copies more or less (more I guess.) Uncle John amused himself after a fashion till about 1 o'clock when he slipped off without saying a word to anyone and didn't come back until about 5. We kept some lunch ready for him for awhile and then had it cleared away, and when Uncle John arrived he wouldn't have anything to eat at all — not eating anything from breakfast-time till dinner-time! In the evening he went off to the "Baptiss meetin," and whether Ted went with him or to our own meeting I don't know. Didn't do very much of anything particular, myself. (Rainy all day.)

Thurs. 10th. Mother had Mrs. Ronne and Blanche to lunch. Mother was somewhat troubled about Uncle John but he considerately stayed in town all day and

had his lunch there, going to Mr. Chipman's to dinner. Nettie came to lunch and stayed till about half-past 4; the others left very soon after lunch. I walked with Mother down to the coffee room and then went in town with Millie and Winnie. Evening wrote out a Puzzle answer ("Harper's Young People"). Bridget leaves us this evening, I don't know whether she has gone yet or not. (Morning beautiful, mild, fine, spring-like day. Walking better.)

Fri. 11th. Bridget did go last night so dish washing "and sich" was in order today. Afternoon escorted Mother to W.C.T.U., and quite late Millie and Winnie came in to see me. I don't think there is anything more to say today. (Morning rained hard. Afternoon cleared, came out quite fine but it was pretty cold.)

Sat. 12th. Uncle John left here this morning very early. Went in town with Millie and Winnie about 11:30. Nettie came in, but only for a few minutes.... Father is getting better and tonight for first time came downstairs to tea. (Very cold, it snowed during the night, covering the ground thinly, but it went off mostly during the day. It sprinkled snow sparingly but to no good.)

Sun. 13th. This was my birthday — no.18. Eighteen birthdays seem a good many to have had, but of them all I remember only one that was an unhappy day; that was my 10th, but what's the good of remembering unpleasant things? This one was a very happy one, and I was glad it came on a Sunday because it seemed only suitable somehow to begin on a fresh year with going to church and that. It always amuses me to wait and see how long it is before anyone remembers it is my birthday and wishes me many happy returns of the day. They usually find it out somehow by breakfast-time and they are always surprised. (My writing is very bad, but that's because I am writing with my desk on my

BARRINGTON STREET   HALIFAX, N.S.

1375

Ladies College, Halifax, N.S.

lap.) I don't remember how they found out this time; I didn't mention that it was my birthday and even refrained from tearing yesterday's date off the calendar. Mother's present to me was a dollar and when I went to wish Papa "Good morning" he had another one for me. Bessie surprised me very much (I needn't say anything about how pleased I was) by presenting me with "Nine Little Goslings," a book I have long wanted. I really think it was so good of her to spend all that money on me — it surely must have cost her a dollar. —— The day was like my usual Sundays; went to church morning, learned hymns afternoon also going for a little walk with Frank when he came home from Sunday School. Papa was well enough to come down to dinner and tea. (Weather was fine, but with high cold wind — real Marchy day it was.)

Mon. 14th. Nettie came in to lunch. Millie came to bring me a birthday present in the shape of a very pretty chiffon bow for the neck, and Winnie came later and brought me a beautiful hyacinth and a piece of music, and a card from Mary. I did not go out at all, which I regretted. Father came down to lunch and dinner. Nothing more I think tonight. (About equally fine and cloudy, with snow squall.)

Tue. 15th. Afternoon I went in town with Bessie; we went to Cragg's and I ordered my vasculum which will cost a whole dollar! Evening went with Mary Gooderson to see a calisthenic exercise at the Ladies' College, in which Winnie took part. It was lovely. (The weather was extremely unpleasant, very cold, dusty; though frozen with a piercing wind.)

Wed. 16th. Nettie came in about lunch time, and about 3:30 or 4 she left to pay some calls. She came back afterwards but I was out then. Dr. Read came in to see Papa.... No one came for me and Bessie and Josie went out together so as there wasn't anyone to go

with me. I went for a walk by myself about 4:30 or 5, for the afternoon was much too fine to be wasted in the house. I went straight up Spring Garden Road to Robie Street, thence over to the Willow Tree and home via Quinpool Road. The walking was very good, mostly frozen. After I came home Millie and Winnie came in to see me but they didn't stay long. I wish I could talk more; I think they find it very dull over here (or more likely it is me they find dull), and sometimes it seems to me as if they dropped in as a sort of duty or politeness, when they have got through with whatever else more entertaining they may have on hand — though I couldn't blame poor Millie today since she spent three hours this afternoon at the dentist! I never seem to be able to say anything that interests them, and after they are gone I have such wretched feelings a sort of mixture of resentfulness, anger with myself and everyone else, and a sort of despair of ever being an object of sincere affection to them — though perhaps I may be doing them a great injustice in feeling that they are not as fond of me as ever. I think Winnie seems fonder of me than Millie. I suppose the root of the whole matter is that I myself am at fault, but I wish to goodness I knew how to fix up things better. And the question just now is: Why on earth was I such a goose as to write all this stuff? I suppose because I am "queer." (Very fine: cold but very pleasant.)

Thurs. 17th. Morning Josie and I went for a walk out Coburg Road, afternoon Millie and Winnie came in to see me. I really don't know anything else to put down — oh, except that I had to entertain Blanche a little while this morning. (Fine, very pleasant; milder, walking quite good.) St. Patrick's Day. There was no procession last night but one this morning.

Fri. 18th. Did nothing very important today. Read a great deal of "Lady Jane" aloud to Papa; we own the book

now as Mother sent to Jim for it. Dishes, some ripping, and piecing for Mother's mat, etc. (Very snowy.)[10]

Sat. 19th. Finished "Lady Jane" aloud to Papa. Josie and Ted are carrying on and it's past my bed time and this is a scratchy pen and I lent Josie my other one and my ink is nearly all used up, and isn't this a pretty picture I have drawn, and *am* I going demented? We'll just put it down to a temporary agitation of an intellect insufficiently supplied with sleep (I have taken to going to bed late lately) and now Ted has captured my diary and has pranced all around the room with it with Josie hanging some of the way to his coat tails (he has grabbed it several times before — hence the smouch — but I always managed to recover it) and now I have got it back (my diary I mean) and I suppose I may as well wind up by saying that I went out by myself for a little while this afternoon and in the evening. Did nothing much but looked through a "Harper's Young People." Goodnight. (Rained blew very hard. Snowed hailed and was fine for a little while afternoon.)

Mon. 21st. Yesterday I went to church morning learned hymns afternoon and read evening. It was as fearfully windy, cold fairly fine with two snow squalls. Today nothing much happened. Nettie was in to lunch. Afternoon about half-past 4 went in to the Library and got a book for myself and one for Josie. I walked some of the way home with Una Gray. I shall not stoop tonight to the foolishness of describing my feelings — anyway, I don't think I understand them myself sufficiently. Perhaps the Equinoctial has got entangled in my buzzam! I shouldn't wonder. (Cold, fairly fine.) Millie and Winnie were in for about three minutes after I got home to ask me to tea to Millie's tomorrow. I hope that Seeton girl won't be there and I hope I shan't be done out when I come home, I feel sort of weak lately.

Tue. 22nd. Afternoon Josie and Bessie went to a 5 o'clock tea at Blanche's, Nettie went too but first came in to see us a little while. About half-past 5 I went to Millie's to tea, and the other guests were: Winnie, Lucy Cady, Una Gray, and Anna Mitchell — a very congenial little company, though I confess I had been afraid that Miss Seeton and Miss Bullock would be of the number too. Millie and Winnie see a great deal of these two as well as a good many others of the set at the rink and also at the club they have, supposed to be a literary club, the chief literary feature being the edition of a paper called "The Girl's Gazette" issued monthly and printed from a real press. This is wandering from Millie's party though. We had a very nice time indeed. We had some charades (at which Una is capital), and Up Jenkins and a little dancing (!). I don't think we played anything else because the charades took up so much of the time. Father went out this morning for the first time since his illness; he did not go to his office but to the Probate Court. (Morning fine, afternoon rather dull; cold, yet I didn't think it unpleasant.)[11]

Wed. 23rd. Nothing particularly marked happened today. I was going in town with Bessie afternoon but the weather was so bad Mother wouldn't let me out. Millie was in for a few minutes. (Morning dull, afternoon snowy, evening real wintery blizzardy storm ending in rain.) Got a new pair of shoes. I add this item so as to see how long I will wear them before having to get another.

Thurs. 24th. Afternoon the girls came in to see me for a little while before they went to the rink. It was not private day but as the rink closes very soon — next week I think — they naturally want to make the best of it while it remains open. After they went, I went out for a walk by myself for as Josie went out with Frank and Bessie was too tired to go out I was obliged to be my own

The Acadian Recorder.

(Established 1813.)

I wonder if anybody except me reads the wonderful receipts for "keeping beautiful forever" which are daily to be found in our papers? I also wonder if anyone is fool enough to try them. For my part, even if I had the desire, I have not the time. What with the lotions, the powders, the oils, and the masks, yes, actually masks, "false faces," wh... going to be... get them... receipt, g... quickly do... face daily... plunge you... soft cloth... toilet soap... briskly wi... cess gone t...

LADY JANE'S LETTER.

A week of interest in Society.

HOW "TO KEEP BEAUTIFUL FOR-EVER."

Personal Fashionable Notes. — The Royal present. — The hateful, noise-less bicycles, etc.

Have you noticed how pretty are the girls of the coming generations? and what lovely hair so many of them have? I would strongly urge those of the present society, who can do so, to marry and make no long tarrying before these young ones come out...

LADY JANE'S LETTER.

The Weddings and the Brides.

ABOUT THE WANDERERS' BAZAAR.

Society in a quiver. — Summer visitors. — Miss Morrow's wedding. — The last Orpheus Concert. — Herr Döring and his Cello, etc.

A more perfect day for excursionists and holiday seekers could not have dawned than Tuesday last, the 24th of May. All Halifax was on the loose, and it is to the unbounded credit of the little city that the police reports state that not a single "drunk"... paragraph... 25th must... temperance... Rocking-... most popular... mantle of his... O'Dell, and... has always... surprising to... the guests... the inside... then one is...

Public Gardens, Halifax, N. S.

A SNAPSHOT OF HALIFAX, N. S.
WITH A TYPICAL CANADIAN GIRL

M. and W. see a great deal of these too as well as a good many others of the set at the rink and also at a club they have, supposed to be a literary club, the chief literary feature being the edition of a paper called "The Girl's Gazette" issued monthly and printed from a real press. This is wandering from M.'s party though. We had a very nice time indeed.

companion. I went out in a very bad temper because Mother didn't want me to go along either Coburg, Jubilee or Quinpool Road but I felt more good-natured by the time I got home. (I am really awfully ill-tempered and irritable lately.) I walked down Tower Road to South Street thence up Robie Street — where I got some odd twigs with seed — vessels remaining on them — and home down Spring Garden Road along by the Gardens. The walking was something really frightful, but with rubber boots I didn't care. Evening I wrote a letter to Mable Fairweather. (Mild, very fine, beautiful day.)

Fri. 25th. Father went in town morning. Afternoon walked with mother to the Coffee Room and then in town with Bessie. Got a picture of the baby from Bert. Blanche was in for awhile evening to say good-bye, goes tomorrow. (Morning fine mild afternoon duller and colder.)

Sat. 26th. Father gave us a tremendous fright this morning by falling about half way down the stairs. He was all ready to go out and his rubbers must have slipped on the stairliner. It was a mercy he was not killed, for he came down head first, and barely escaped striking the radiator. I think he is the most marvellous man to go through so many accidents and come out of them all alive, and he was not even hurt this time except some bruises about the knees. He went in to town just the same as if nothing happened. Afternoon went out for a walk by myself, Spring Garden Road, Robie Street, home South Street and Tower Road. Millie and Winnie came in for a little while about 5 o'clock or so; they had been to a meeting or something of their club. They are preparing for a play, so haven't much time on hand. Received tickets for an entertainment at the Ladies' College which Lidy very kindly sent me. Wrote a note to thank her evening but there was no one to take it so it had to wait until Sunday. (Fairly fine, mild.)

Sun. 27th. As usual, church morning (Mr. Rogers preached) afternoon hymns — 50. (Fine colder.)

Mon. 28th. After getting through with dishes, and practising, I got ready and went to take my note to Alida. After that I kept on down Barrington Street, went to Cragg's, got my vasculum, and paid for it. It is a big beauty, though the opening was not made as I intended but it will do just as well as it is and certainly is more conveniently wide. After lunch I varnished the soles of a pair of my boots. Stayed in afternoon and wrote a letter to Mrs. Bolster to thank her for cards she sent me. Evening Ted, Bess, and I went to see the entertainment at the Ladies' College. We thought we were in lots of time, but when we got there the hall was nearly full and we were obliged to content ourselves with a back seat where we couldn't see well at all. Still we saw enough to be delighted with the whole affair, of which I have saved a pro-gramme. I meant to describe the prettiest things but I don't believe I can. The two "moving tableaux" were lovely. "Mary" danced in and watered her living flowers in the most charming manner, to the music of the song sung behind the scenes. The "Days of the Week" also kept time to music but some did it better than others. "Monday's child" came in admiring herself in a hand glass. "Tuesday" just glided about gracefully — she was Mable Fairweather's friend, Louise Holden — "Wednesday" was gay with a skip-ping rope; but "Thursday's child" was best of all. She came in dressed all in black with a most woe-begone expression and when she got to the centre of the plat-form she mopped her eyes most pathetically. "Friday" was not such a success, she came in too stiffly and looked too proud to be "loving and giving." Her emblem was a basket filled with things for the poor I suppose. "Saturday" was very good; she was dressed in black with a white apron, a basket on her arm, and was sewing busily as she passed along. "Sunday" I did

PROGRAMME.

1. CHORUS—Barcarolle Fidelin........................ .... *Brahms.*

2. "MARY, MARY, QUITE CONTRARY."
   Mary....................................MISS MAGGIE MCKENZIE.
   Pretty Maids all in a row ....MISS ALICE PUTNAM,
      MISS GERTRUDE SKINNER,   MISS ELLA HILLSON,
      MISS BESSIE ROBERTSON,   MISS EVA HOLMES.
   Flowers ....MISS KATIE GORDON,   MISS DOTTIE HOLMES,
      MISS AIJDA SEAMAN,   MISS FLORENCE ELLIS,
      MISS MAUDE BISHOP,   MISS ELLA MONTAGUE.

3. DAYS OF THE WEEK.
   Monday's child is fair of face....................... ......MISS ALICE GRAHAM.
   Tuesday's child is full of grace.....................MISS LOUISE HOLDEN.
   Wednesday's child is joyous and glad...............MISS ANNIE CAMPBELL.
   Thursday's child is sorry and sad.....................MISS EDNA MCKENZIE.
   Friday's child is loving and giving ....MISS BERTA SMITH.
   Saturday's child has to work for a living ....MISS CHRISTIE FRASER.
   But the child that is born on the Sabbath day
   Is bonnie and blithe and good and gay...............MISS ADA WILLIAMS.

4. PIANO—Aubade .... *Kevning.* ~~Think I would like to get this piece.~~
      MISS KATIE GORDON.

5. VIOLIN—Allegro vivace, Sonate in D Major, Op. 137 .... *Schubert.*
      MISS BEATRICE WHIDDEN.

6. RECITATION—The Ruggles's Dinner....... ... *Kate Douglas Wiggin.*
      MISS CLARA ROSBOROUGH.

7. VIOLIN —When the Swallows Homeward Fly..............*Schroeder.*
      MISS EDNA MACKENZIE.

8. PIANO—Fantasie ....*Gustav Lange.*
      MISS FLORENCE JAMESON.

PART II.

PETITE COMEDIE EN DEUX ACTES.

PAR LE REV. F. W. BOUVERIE.

ÒÙ SONT DONC CES MESSIEURS?

Personnages :

Madame De La Vieille-Roche ....MLLE. EDITH SKINNER.
Mesdemoiselles Virginie ....MLLE. EVA HOLMES.
  "   Heloïse } Ses filles ....MLLE. HATTIE LAWRENCE.
  "   Corinne } ....MLLE. GEORGIE HADDOW.
Aglaé (femme de chambre) ....MLLE. BESSIE ROBERTSON.
Mesdemoiselles Violante De Crève-Court............MLLE. ENID MACLEAN.
  "   Agnès De La Belle-Source.........MLLE. BERTA SMITH.
  "   Candide De La Franchise..........MLLE. LOUISE HOLDEN.
  "   Diane Du Haut-Ton,........ MLLE. ALICE GRAHAM.
Les Messieurs (qui ne viennent pas) :
M. Le Vicomte De La Tour—Fermée:
M. Le Chevalier D'Outremer.
M. Le Capitaine De L'Etoile.
M. Le Baron De La Honte.

PIANO—Polka (Bohenn) .... *Rubenstein.*
   MISS BEATRICE SALTER.
PIANO—Phantasie (First Movement) ....*Mendelssohn.*
   MISS BESSIE ROBERTSON.

GOD SAVE THE QUEEN!

not think very good, she was in black with a Bible. I suppose it was, but though she looked "good" she didn't look "bonnie, blithe and gay." Little Katie Gordon played very well on the piano and so did Beatrice Whiddon on the violin. The next two pieces I liked very much too, but I didn't care very much for the eighth. The "comedie" was capital — though I fear I should never have guessed what it was all about if it had not been explained in English first. They rattled off the French as if it was their native language, and the acting, *when* we could see it (!) was capital. Altogether it was a very good entertainment indeed, and I enjoyed it greatly. (Rather dull, with cold high wind.)

Tue. 29th. Afternoon Mother, Josie and I drove out to see Nettie. The Grays also came out to see her so Mother went home with them as our man could not come for us till late, so Josie and I had the carriage to ourselves. Mrs. Hart took Bessie to an Orpheus Concert evening. She took Josie last time. (Though not very fine at first, it turned out a lovely day and the evening was simply exquisite with a dainty new moon and Venus in the west.)

Wed. 30th. Afternoon Millie was in for a few minutes before going to her rehearsal. Then I went for a walk by myself; down to the end of South Park Street then down the road a little way as far as the brook where I lingered for a few minutes hoping to find some botanical specimens but found nothing worth bringing home. I did not think it right to go further so turned back but after going the length of Park Street I branched off up Spring Garden Road, along Summer Street and Sackville Street, home Park Street Anna Mitchell came to the door to ask me to tea to her house tomorrow night. (Beautifully sunny day, but cold, dusty with high wind.)

Thurs. 31st. It's a good thing that this is the last day of March for already I have stretched out my daily records over seven or eight pages. In the future I am afraid I must abbreviate more or I will have exhausted my book before the year is out. I did a good deal this day; morning helped Mother and Bessie take some things for a W.C.T.U. Bazaar down to the Masonic Hall; afternoon went to the bazaar with Josie and Lucy Macdonald; then came home and hurried to get dressed; went over for Winnie, went with her and Lidy to tea at Anna Mitchell's. There were quite a number there; Millie and Lucy, we three, Lucy Harrington, Lida Mott, Birdie Salter, Edie Anderson, Beata Stairs, Lalia Graham, Dollie Harvey and I think that was all. Had a very nice time though I was awfully shy at first and no doubt looked an awkward clown. Had mind reading and Clubs. Came home with Winnie and Company. (Beautifully fine, though rather cold and dusty.)

April

Fri. 1st. Nettie came in to lunch, and afterwards I went in town with her. Wallace fooled her greatly this morning (1st April!) so she was bound to get even with him and got me to write him a note supposed to come from Mrs. Leigh (or Lee) saying she would let him have her house (she has put such a high rent on it that they can't take it.) I did not do much fooling, I wanted to give someone a real good bang up fool but I couldn't think of anything suitable and I had to resort to sewing the knives and forks to the table cloth, which was a little fun, not much. (Another lovely day, very much warmer, almost hot.)

Sat. 2nd. Morning Josie went out to stay with Lucy Macdonald. Afternoon I took my solitary constitutional, Morris, Robie and South Streets Bessie and I were going to the park but Maggie had a bad headache and went to bed, so we couldn't go. She was better by tea time and able to help with the dishes. Evening Ted took Bessie to a sacred concert given by the band of the Leicestershire regiment; I wanted to go but was not asked so stayed home and wrote this. I thought I'd got over my blues, but tonight I feel nearly as doleful as ever. Oh, fie! cheer up, girl. Beautiful day, very like yesterday. It was so warm that when out I took off my fur collar and carried it the rest of the way home.

Sun. 3rd. Went to church evening. Mr. Moore, as usual. (Another glorious hot day.)

Mon. 4th. Josie came home early this morning. Helped Mother and Bessie with some things, I mean they cleaned the china closet and I wiped some dishes. After lunch I escorted Father to the barber's on Queen Street and walked up and down till he came out and walked home with him. Then a while afterward I took my usual lonely walk, this time I ventured down the lane that runs down off South Street. Got some "little periopanopigus Agasagasagagay" as Frank calls my botanical specimens — this time it was that little rock flower which I think now is a kind of cinquefoil. My demon hung around me today a great deal more than I liked. Alas, baleful melancholy, how shall I get the mastery over you? I do wonder why I am so crazy and what shall I do to help it? (Fine as ever and oh! so warm! Quite warm enough to leave off my coat even dispensing with a thinner one, but I didn't take it off. I am always shy at first of going without.)

Tue. 5th. Josie went with Miss B. MacGregor out to Nettie's to lunch and didn't get home until we were nearly through dinner. Took my walk today past Mr. Stairs to see his crocuses which are in fine array of bloom. My bad demon made me pretty grumpy, and I even shed some well ordered tears in a quiet nook after dinner as an accompaniment to Josie's playing on the piano.

Wed. 6th. Pretty much the same routine as usual. Nettie was in to lunch. Afternoon took my walk around Summer Street, College Street, Robie Street, Jubilee Road as far as the cemetery gate where I turned in and sat me down to meditate. It was just lovely in there, the air so very sweet and soothing with a pleasant little cool wind, and there were some sweet little birds singing there, linnets I think. I concluded I would come here often but somewhat to my surprise Mother forbade me to go again when I told here where I had been. I saw pussy willows in blossom and the grass too is growing so bright and green among the stalks of last year's growth.

OAKLANDS, NORTH WEST ARM   HALIFAX, N.S.

1373 S

I ventured down the lane that runs down off South St. Got some "little periopinopigus Agasagasagapay" as I calls my botanical specimens, this time. it was that little rock-flower which I think now is a kind of cinquefoil. My demon hung around me today a great deal more than I liked. Alas, baleful melancholy, how shall I get the mastery over you?

Felt better today, I was only gloomy in spots, and tried to rid myself of them. I think I would feel better if I could understand my own feelings, express them accurately and, most important of all, have someone to whom I could tell them who would understand me and sympathize. There is not one I know who I feel would comprehend what I mean and know what to say to me, so Diary, I have to come to you, and I shouldn't wonder if it did me good to unburden my soul even this much and although I may laugh at my own silliness when reading it over. I daresay if I keep on at this rate I shall be at the end of the book before half of the year is out, but I don't care, I shall manage somehow. Well I must not waste time and paper on more of this trash, but go wash my hair, which is a job I hate. (Very fine, rather cool wind.)

Thurs. 7th. A week since Anna's party and since I have seen my (once) constant chums. And the moral of it is? — Don't put your trust in friendship, for when you grow cranky and dull and stupid you may be deserted, and then what does your friendship amount to? I know *one* thing, I don't want to go to their old play and I shan't if I can get out of it. There! Am I not getting to be a nice pleasant spiteful thing. Let's bear away and get on to today's happenings. Morning much the same as usual, afternoon too. Went for my walk Park Street and Tower Road as far down as the older thicket. (Very fine, but dusty with high cold wind.)

Fri. 8th. Thrilling and noteworthy event! Actually saw Millie and Winnie for a few minutes!!!! Met them near the cemetery gate and walked home with them. I walked out to Mr. Cunningham's to return a basket (which Mr. Cunningham had left at the house with eggs in it) and while I was gone a great masonic funeral passed. I was sorry not to have a good look at it so afterwards Frank and I went out towards the cemetery hoping to see it coming back. We saw the chief fea-

tures, some aproned and otherwise decorated creatures among them six or eight dressed in long white cloaks with red crosses on the side and crusaders' caps. They were Knights Templars I suppose and they *did* look funny. (Fine mostly but with chilly wind.)

Sat. 9th. Stayed in with Mother while Bessie and Josie were out, though I did go as far as Horseman's on an errand. (The weather was cold, raw and dull, began to rain soon after 5 p.m. and *kept up steadily*.)

Sun. 10th. Morning church and afterwards went for a walk with Ted. Met Josie and Lucy on Quinpool Road by the Common and walked back as far as the Willow Tree with them, then Josie came home with us. Afternoon hymns, per usual, and also escorted Father on a short walk to the end of the Gardens and back again. (Weather was all sorts of funny things; was fine and sunny, was cold and windy; was dull and rainy and also snowy. Fickle April!)

Mon. 11th. Nettie was in to lunch. Afternoon walked down the Park Road as far as the stone wall, mooned around there a little and then came home the same way. (Very high cold windy, dusty, fairly fine, at times very fine.)

Tue. 12th. Spent the day with Nettie. About 11 o'clock Bessie and I went into Mahon's, and there took the car as far as they go, then walked out Chebucto Road to Nettie's. After lunch when Nettie was playing for us on the piano, Frank very unexpectedly put in an appearance and stayed and walked home with us. Mrs. Jordan, Mrs. Oxley, Mrs. Jones all drove out to see Nettie and brought Constance and Beresford with them. I ran outdoors with the children and showed them the brook and kept them amused till the others went. Then we started for home, Nettie walking a little way with us. (Awfully windy and dusty and cold. Fairly fine.)

After lunch when N. was playing for us on the piano Frank very unexpectedly put in an appearance & staid & walked home with us. Mrs. Jordan, Mrs. Oxley, Mrs. Jones all drove out to see N. & brought Constance & Beresford with them.

Wed. 13th. Morning escorted Father to the Court House. Afternoon Mother went over to speak to Mary about a washerwoman and I went to see Winnie for a few minutes. She has been miserable with a cold. Blues made me wriggle mentally. Not very fine, cold. I have not yet wished to dispense with my winter coat except those first very warm days, while this time last year I think I was wearing my spring jacket.

Thurs. 14th. Afternoon Mother and I went up to Harris's to see his annual Easter display. No comment is needed where flowers are concerned! Quite late Winnie
came to see me. (Fair, not
particularly fine, still quite
cool and dusty.)

Fri. 15th. This was Good
Friday and the weather was
anything but good. We had
some hot cross buns last night
for tea, the first we have had
for ever so long, longer than I
can remember. I stayed home
this morning with Father,
while all the rest were at
church. Afternoon had out
my scrapbook. (Morning dull,
cold. Afternoon very *snowy*.)

Sat. 16th. Afternoon in town with Bessie to see about a new spring hat for me. Then went for a walk by myself, Tower Road and South Park Street. Nothing particular happened. Didn't feel blue at all today I think; happily! (Fine, much warmer, wind cool though.)

Sun. 17th. Church morning and then walked up the street a bit with Mother. Afternoon hymns and another stroll with Father. This was Easter Sunday and there were beautiful flowers in church. (Only fairly fine; rather cold.)

Mon. 18th. What happened today? Oh yes, Mother, Father, Frank and I drove out to Nettie's and brought her home to lunch. I read "The First Violin" nearly all day. Ted came home from Berwick evening. Had about as bad a fit of the blues as I have had yet. Ah, me! (Finer afternoon than morning; it snowed a bit morning.)

Tue. 19th. Winnie came in at lunch time to tell me
that Millie was ill and
wanted me to come and see
her, so I went down and
was quite awhile there.
She's been ill a week, up for
the first time today. (Only
"fair to middling," coldish.)

Wed. 20th. Afternoon went
for an aimless sort of walk
with Bessie and Frank. We
crossed Camp Hill and
came home Robie Street
way. After we got home,
Millie and Winnie dropped
in to see me. This is Mabel
Hall's wedding day. Dr.
MacMurdo is her future
husband. This pen is abom-
inable! (Beautifully fine, warm too.)

Thurs. 21st. Morning Josie and I went down to the Park and were there quite awhile; we went and came in the cars. We went to Chain Battery and sat there by the shore. (Gloriously fine and warm. Put on my last year's spring jacket but found even that too much and took it off.)

Fri. 22nd. Nothing much happened. It rained hard.

Grafton St. Methodist Church, Halifax, N.S.

Sun. 17th Church mrng. & then walked up the street a bit with
with Mother. Aftn. hymns & another stroll with Father. This
was Easter, & there were beautiful flowers in church. (Only fairly fine — rather cold.)

Mother and Bessie housecleaned the nursery. I read "Last Days of Pompeii" and Josie read a lot of it aloud to me too. This is a new pen but it is not much better than the old.

Sat. 23rd. Josie's birthday; gave her nothing but many happy returns. Bessie gave her a cup and saucer. Afternoon went to Buckley's and got a sponge and to Horneman's and got some hat elastic. Also went for a walk by myself out Quinpool Road way thinking to meet and walk back with Josie, who had walked out with Lucy; what was my amazement then, to see them both vanish into a cab and drive off!! She came back after tea though. Millie and Winnie were in awhile. (Rainy morning, cleared afternoon but went foggy again.)

Sun. 24th. Church (Mr. Johnson), hymns and a walk with Josie after Sunday School. (Fine, but cold and windy, steam rising in clouds off the streets.)

Mon. 25th. Mr. Barry whitewashed the halls, and carpet being off the stairs the noise is horrible. Fact is, I'm nervous and I hardly ever touch tea, too. Afternoon walk by myself, around by the College and Morris Street etc. (Fine, still chilly though the sun was warm.)[12]

Tue. 26th. Didn't go out; had a cold and sore throat. So had Frank, only worse and went to bed. Sat by the fire and did nothing the whole afternoon. Morning I trimmed over a hat. Winnie was in for a few minutes afternoon. (Fine, very.)

Wed. 27th. Very much like yesterday; loafed indoors all day. Frank pretty sick, with a rash out. Mother fearing scarlet fever sent for the doctor afternoon. He said it was not scarlet fever; great relief in the Shannon family, for we didn't relish the idea of placards and quarantine. Bessie and Josie and Ted have sore throats too! (Very fine and bright.)

Thurs. 28th. If I kept a "dot calendar" I think I should speckle this day pretty blackly, for I had to see Dr. Read all by myself and tell him things that still make me cruddle with disgust. Then too, poor old Frank is worse than he thought in that he has scarlet rash which is like a very mild scarlet fever. We won't have to be placarded the doctor says, but we'd better stay at home and not go to meetings etc. If we have to be semi-quarantined it seems to one Frank might as well have it thoroughly at once so that he will be less likely to get it again! I shan't be able to see the girls' play now, though Ted is still bound to go. (Fine morning, afternoon dull.)

Fri. 29th. Loafed indoors and did nothing worth mentioning. Doctor came, didn't see me this time! Frank doing well. Ted had to go to the bank evening so couldn't go to see the girls' play, neither could any of us. (Rainy nearly all day, alas.)

Sat. 30th. Morning about the same as usual, only the girls came over to tell me about their play. Mother wouldn't let them in, though; she didn't tell them about Frank but gave the excuse that I had a sore throat and couldn't talk to them — and to be sure, I am more "Darding Bary Jade"-y than I think I was ever before. Well, the girls seemed delighted with their entertainment and said it was a great success. I should like to hear what else they have to say about it. There were to be two plays, "Bluebeard" and one all about flowers, some tableaux and I think some music but I am not sure. I asked Ted if any of the young men at the bank went and he said yes and I asked him what they thought of it, and he said they didn't think much of it; "it was pretty good for 'little girls', but Ted didn't miss much by not going!" So much for different opinions! — — Afternoon had a great and important conference with Dr. Read, ugh! Guess that is all for today. (Rainy most all day, though it cleared a little afternoon.)

May

Sun. 1st. Went not out, read morning, learned a hymn (60th) and looked out of the drawing room window afternoon. Nettie was in for a few minutes evening. She said she wasn't a bit afraid of scarlet fever. Gardens opened today. (Fine but cold).

Mon. 2nd. Got "Popular Science News" for May and it had an extract from one of my reports in it, but he had changed it! Not the sense, of course, but the way it was worded, though I must confess I like my own way best! However, I suppose he had to do it to get it in at all, but I'd as soon it had been left out! It made me quite mortified and upset for a little while! Didn't go out. I was in town and got me a new scribbler so I tried evening to scribble a report. The bimonthly nightmare's begun!! (Rainy morning, dull afternoon.)

Tue. 3rd. Stayed indoors and Winnie was in for a little while to see me. She was full of their play (which is to be repeated at the Blind Asylum for the benefit of the blind children) and described it all graphically. She also told us about Minnie winning a tricycle at the matinée on Saturday, which made us laugh till the tears came. (Rainy I think. Anyway it was not fine.)

Wed. 4th. Frank not so well today and poor Bessie caved in at last with the quinsey. She has fought it off bravely, but couldn't forever. Millie was in awhile afternoon. Drawing room all upset, housecleaning! (Rainy again!)[13]

Thurs. 5th. Was out for the first time for a good while, and glad enough to get out too. Escorted Mother in town to Dr. Merrill's among other places and she expects to get her teeth on Saturday. After leaving her at the Coffee Room, I came home and then went over to the Gardens. Frank better, poor Bess very bad, almost speechless. (Very fine but with high wind, dusty.)

Fri. 6th. Morning helped about the housecleaning, just minor things you know, yet I think I worked harder than I have ever done before, since a good while anyway. (Any mistakes must be put down to its being late and I being tired and it's Saturday evening I'm writing.) Well, I went over to Winnie's about half-past 6 and she and Millie and I had a little informal tea in the drawing room as the dining room was being cleaned, and then they two went off to prepare for their entertainment at the Blind Asylum and I came a little later with Mary and Ed Dwyer. We were there when the doors were opened and got splendid seats, right in the front row, only a little too near the band which they played during the intervals. The whole affair was just splendid. Millie looked simply lovely in a cream-coloured dress with bunches of violets. She was splendid and so was Winnie as the King, indeed I think the King was better than Millie. Scarlet Runner was too funny for anything and Lidy Mott was capital as Prince Coxcont. Lalia Graham did very well too and looked very nice all in blue. After "Mignonette" there was a tableaux of the "Seasons" and then "Bluebeard." Lidy Mott was better than ever and

Programme

FRIDAY, MAY 6, 1892.

I. FAIRY TALE DRAMA. "MIGNONETTE; OR, THE FAIRY VERVAIN'S SPELL."

DRAMATIS PERSONAE.

King Tigerlily, (Monarch of Awleservaise.) .... Miss Winnie Burns.
Cocksco... of Fiddle-de-dee. ...... Chevalier. } Suitors to the Princess Violet.
Eglanti... ...... } ...... Miss Ella Seeton.

Count ......

John ......
Daffy ......
Scar... ......
Prin... ......

Bl... ......
Da... ......
A2 ......
Fairy ......
Duchess Cabbage-leaf, ...

PUBLIC GARDENS   HALIFAX, N.S.

ACT I.

SCENE I. Boudoir of the Princess Violet.
SCENE II. The same.

ACT II.

SCENE I. The same.
SCENE II. A room of State in the Castle.

II. TABLEAU.—THE SEASONS.

Spring .... Miss F. Anderson.
Summer .... Miss C. Story.
.... Miss F. Seeton.
...... Miss L. Graham.

Lucy Harrington was a splendid Fatima. It was all splendid and I liked it very much indeed and after I'd said I wasn't going to their play too! And it was so kind of Winnie to take me. Well! I must go to bed now, and leave Saturday till Monday!

Sat. 7th. What happened this day? Oh yes, the girls were in for a while morning. Afternoon went with Mother in the tram down town. Went to the dentist's and she got her new teeth and then we saw Andrew's carriage there so we drove out to Nettie's little new house on the Mumford Road — or off of it. It has a horrid situation, I think, though they have a pretty view of the Basin. There is a dreadful avenue up to it. It looks as if it went through a potato field with some wretched little young trees scattered over it. Inside the house isn't so bad. It is very small and real country, but Nettie has some pretty furniture and has arranged it very prettily. I didn't want to go home very much, and Nettie said "Never mind, wait till she got her spare bedroom fixed up." Now, do you suppose she'll have me to stay out with her? I would like to very much but I'll be much surprised if she asks me, "*nicht wahr?*" Evening I laboured over a report to Agassiz Association, finally finished it...good enough! Guess nothing else happened. (Very cold and disagreeable, dull and showery.)

Sun. 8th. Don't know why I wrote that, for nothing particular happened. So cold I had to go back to my winter jacket. (Cold, windy.)

Mon. 9th. Didn't go out. Helped about the house and worked a bit among my botanical affairs and read a little. (The weather was dreadful, cold and windy and dusty.)

Tue. 10th. Dishes, ironing, dusting, flower pressing and a little studying in botany, morning but didn't kill myself with hard work in any of these departments!

After went to the Library for a book for Josie. Nettie was in for a short visit. Bessie is well now and picking up her affairs about the house. (Very fine, warmer.)

Wed. 11th. Morning went in town with Papa to the Legislative Library. Postman left me a letter from some unknown personage which caused quite a little commotion when read. It was from some John Legro, of Montreal, whose great great grandfather was Capt. Crane, about whom he wished information. This was owing (I mean my getting this letter) to Mr. Legro's seeing my name in last "Popular Science News," so he thought he would write me, but he didn't send a stamp for return! Afternoon took a walk by myself, Spring Garden Road to Robie Street to corner of Camp Hill, across and home through the Gardens. Got houstonia on Camp Hill. Nothing particular happened, besides, I think I'm getting moody again. I *do* miss Millie and Winnie, I used to see *so* much of them. (Fine morning. Afternoon dull, cold, raw.)

Life is like a leaf I cried: Like a leaf the echoing rocks replied.

Thurs. 12th. I should have gone out, but I had no one to go with, nowhere to go and I wasn't sure if it was going to rain again so I loafed indoors. Tonight I feel every bit as blue as ever I did. This is Nettie's birthday. (Weather morning rainy, foggy. Afternoon brightened and finally cleared up.)

Fri. 13th. Afternoon escorted Father over to the Gardens. Came home and read the rest of the time and after dinner went with Mother to see Miss Crane to try to find out something about that Capt. Crane Mr. Legro asked about. Didn't gain much information though. Evening made some copies of a letter to John I. Legro, Esq. (Beautifully fine and much warmer. Went back to spring jacket.)

The Popular Science News
AND
BOSTON JOURNAL OF CHEMISTRY.

AN A. A. OBSERVER IN HALIFAX.

My plan of work has been a little different from last year's. I have been studying the plants more closely, and while before I only copied out the analysis from my book, I now write out a full description, including my own observations. Then I sketch all the most important parts of the whole plant, and when both sketches and description are completed they are ready to be placed in a book

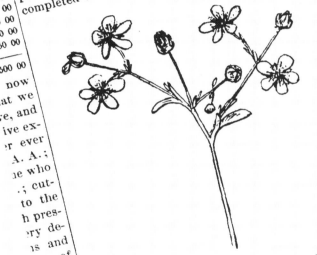

kept for the purpose. I send you as a sample a copy of my first completed set of sketches. The plant is *Potentilla tridentata*, which grows here very abundantly, particularly in rocky places. It has a delicate little white blossom and glossy dark green leaves, which turn red and yellow in the autumn. I kept some specimens in water last spring, and they grew quite well, putting out leaves, roots, and flowers. In the fields it blossomed late in May, and was still in bloom in August.

Yours faithfully,

KATIE W. SHANNON.

$457 75

$ 400 00
400 00
400 00
150 00
150 00

$1500 00

History of the Wedge or A Sketch from Life !!!!

Sat. 14th. The most notable events of the morning: we had a short visit from Nettie and Frank got up and left his semi-quarantine behind him. After, Mother, Father, Bess and I drove out to Nettie's and took her some of her house plants — oh yes, and I posted my letter to Monsieur Legro. This is the last day of a week in which I did not see the girls once to speak to, though I have seen them from the window too often for my peace of mind! I think now I'll just write down how I feel about Millie and Winnie — that is, if I can analyze my feelings sufficiently to express them in words. I know it will use up a lot of space, but I think when the separation is complete I may be curious as to how I felt during the slow process and besides, I should think when a girl has bound as many books as I have, that she ought to be able to paste in some extra foolscap sheets if her diary gets used up before the end of the year.

Well then: I think for a good time I have felt in a vague sort of way (rather than acknowledged) that some day we would grow away from each other, not separated by any actual quarrel but just naturally as our tastes and occupations diverged. But I was quite happy, quite contented, to let matters remain as they were just as long as possible without troubling myself much about what might occur later on. Perhaps the *shadow of the wedge* may have been Millie's going to school, because there she met with other companions and others interests than what were mutual to us both. This was hardly (at all) noticeable when she went to Miss Forbes's but only after she had been going to the [Ladies'] College awhile. I do not speak of Winnie here because I think she was away at this time. I remember Millie's saying to me when Winnie was on the way to Halifax that "she hoped she wouldn't be jealous" when Winnie came because of our being such friends.

Afterwards I thought she was hardly the one to hope to be kept from jealousy! I don't think when Millie and Winnie went to the College together that there was much density to the shadow, for we three seemed just to be happy together. What a long story I am making of all this! Never mind, I mean to go through with it to the end, whether that finds me in tears or on the fifth page from this. I am only afraid that I am writing incoherently or disconnectedly, but I think my memory will supply what links may have slipped my pen. Of course, Millie and Winnie were fond of each other, their natures assimilated better than either mine and Winnie's or mine and Millie's, I think. Yet for a good while, I don't remember now since how long, we were mutually pleased — Millie and I — to tell each other that we loved each other better than Winnie or any other friend. Well I think the real wedge — only the faintest touch of the thinnest edge, yet for all that a reality! — came when Millie went to the rink. Yet, that was only two days out of six, and the other four days I generally was with her; besides, the rink was only during the winter. But what with the rink and school, Millie's acquaintances grew and she was asked to parties, which in her callow youth she has been wont to say she knew she would never care to go to! I don't remember very well how things went after that. I think I gradually began to comprehend, from trifling circumstances, that Winnie favoured Millie rather than me. I suppose I would understand better just how the wedge pierced in if I were to read my diary, vol.2, right through, but that is about as much as my eyes are worth and they are nearly exhausted now. We hardly noticed how the wedge worked in, so gentle was its manipulation — I doubt if either of the girls are more than dimly aware of its presence now! For it has gone in most quickly during a late period, and I know it is not up to its base yet.

(To be continued some time when it's not so late and my eyes are not so tired.)

Perhaps the shadow of the wedge may have been M.'s going to school, because there she met with other companions and other interests than what were mutual to us both. This was hardly (if at all) noticable when she went to Miss Forbes's, but only after she had been going to the college awhile.

Mon. 16th. Girls were in a few minutes this afternoon. (Morning rainy; afternoon dull.)

The Wedge, continued

I think last winter ('91), I was really made aware of the wedge. Millie and Winnie were at the rink so much and I saw so little of them. But after the rink closed matters mended a good bit and the wedge hardly irritated me. When Winnie had her carriage she used often to take Millie and me out driving but Millie came up a great deal for me so she would ask us both together. Then I went away and then Winnie went away. After I came home I used to see Millie pretty often but by no means every day for she went very often over to bathe at the Bullock's place across the Arm. And after Winnie came home she used to go there too. I was therefore very thankful that I had the dear Baby to take over to the Gardens, and what am I going to do this summer without her is more than I can say or even attempt to calculate. Dear Baby! I do wish she were here again! Well, after Nettie's wedding Jamie Rand was staying with us so the girls didn't come very often, but when she had gone I saw more of them for awhile, especially when Millie was preparing for the bazaar.[14] Then we used to prepare for Christmas together, too, but it seems to me that I felt the wedge tighten in just here a bit, for I think the girls would go off together, sometimes, coming in perhaps quite late in the afternoon to see me. I think I must have begun to see by this time that they were fonder of each other than of me, but I don't know, I don't quite remember. I tried, if I did see, not to think much of it or to be jealous and at times I hardly knew the difference. Then Millie started to go to Miss Almon's School and what with the rink and that I saw little enough of either of them. They got up their "Girls Club" and though Winnie did not go to Miss Almon's she went to the rink and soon was a member of the club. Then they started that notion of the play and then it was, I think, that the most decided change in our intercourse took place. Up to this time, I think (I don't remember very well, but I think) Millie when she honoured me with a visit would come up here to the house and then we would go for Winnie first and either not come here at all or else they two would come in quite late and sit and talk awhile. No more nice long walks to the Park, or in Town even. I don't think I have walked along the street with either of them for months except once when we met them the day of the masonic funeral. I fondly hoped that matters would be better when that old play was over, but indeed I think they are worse, for then I knew they were at meetings generally if they didn't come to see me, but now I see them driving and walking together, with never a thought of how I miss them I suppose. I do hope I am not jealous. I would hate to be jealous, it's so wrong, and so uncomfortable. I don't think I hate, oh I know I don't hate them because they seem not to care to have me with them any more and I thought when you were jealous you hated the person. They do come in sometimes and when I am with them they seem just the same as ever towards me, but somehow they just seem to feel better without me I suppose, and besides the carriage is rather small for three. I have a very great sympathy for that poor girl who sang "Oh-h-h-h! Jamie's words went to my heart, There's n-a-e room for twa!"

Oh, I forgot to say when I had certain proof of Millie's changed feelings. It was that night at Anna's and we all

Dingle, Hx.   AP Bruce

agreed we would answer with perfect truth any questions that might be asked those whom the number fell upon. Well, the number fell to Millie, and they asked her who was her favourite girl friend? She answered almost immediately "Winnie." You see I had felt it before and now it had been most unexpectedly proved to me. Afterwards, it is true, she came to me and said she hoped I wasn't offended, that she was afraid I might be, but her eye just fell on Winnie as she sat near her and she just said her name — I wasn't hurt, was I? Of course I set her mind to rest on that score but I guess pretty well that she would have said "Winnie" under any circumstances. I am glad though, that I had found it out before or I am afraid I would have been very much hurt. And I do feel so queer over the whole affair. I feel as it there is a sort of barrier between us now — so there is, the thickness of the wedge — though sometimes I don't feel it so much when I am with them. I feel it most when I see them walking or driving together about the time of the afternoon when I used to go with them and then I feel so strangely, as if I did not want them to come near me after they got through their walk or drive and I get to feel almost broken-hearted sometimes and actually weep some private tears now and again; sometimes I feel almost bitter and then again a pang will come over me almost like physical pain. Well I don't think there's anything more now to write, only to *feel* , and I suppose I'll get used to the new state of things in time. I am only thankful that the change came gradually and not all at once, I think it would have knocked me up completely. I do wish I could be sure I wasn't jealous. I do feel a sort of wounded, hurt, feeling and a very lonely, long, wistful feeling but I think—

Have just had a good talk over it with Josie and I feel much better and sort of cleared up. I didn't mean to let out what I meant when I asked her how it felt to be jealous, but she's sharp, you know, and cute! While I can hardly keep a secret even at Christmas, so she soon got it out of me and I don't think I'm sorry. (I am almost sorry I've written all this stuff though.) We've come to the conclusion that I *am* a little jealous but that Millie and Winnie are still fond of me and by-and-by they will appreciate me more than when they are so much among the other girls. Guess that's all, if I think of anything else I'll have to write across. So no more at present of this morbid confession.

The End.

Tue. 17th. The burning question of the hour just now is: "Have you seen the vampire?" This is by reason of a distinguished visitor who appeared on this date. It happened that I was at the door getting the milk when a well-dressed gentleman came in with a bag and a large black-covered affair, and waited till I could attend to him. Then he enquired if, "I would not like to see a *vampire?* It was not for sale, but only to look at." Well, in the confusion of the moment I hadn't the faintest idea what a vampire was. I knew it was some dreadful tropical creature but whether it was a snake or not I really could not remember. So I said very doubtfully "I — don't know" and next thing, there he was, in the hall, putting down his baggage and uncovering his cage — a fine bright brass one with black plush all round the bottom of it. Well, it was the greatest looking, that vampire! Just like the pictures of bats. While the man was putting down his things Maggie put in an appearance to take the peeling bucket and as the milkman was just going, the strange man arrested him: "*Milkman!* Don't you want to come in and look at this vampire?" or words to that effect. So the milkman, Maggie and I formed a wondering audience about the cage while the owner rehearsed the peculiarities of his pet. Then Mother peered over the bannisters and asked, in some surprise, what it was. I said, "It's a vampire." "Who does it

Entrance to Point Pleasant Park, Halifax, N.S.

Then he brought to light a box of soap
made from this tree which will clean kid gloves wonderfully
& remove spots from cloth.

belong to?" "It belongs to this gentleman" I said, somewhat embarrassed — (in fact, I was afraid she wouldn't like my having let him in, knowing her antipathy to agents). Then she came down and became very much interested in it. Frank, who had had his breakfast in bed, hearing such interesting sounds from below, hurried into his clothes and came to swell the group by the radiator — I think the milkman had gone by this time. Then the man produced a curious looking thing, remarking that he presumed that we had often heard of the soap tree and that was piece of its bark. Then he brought to light a box of soap made from this tree which will clean kid gloves wonderfully and remove spots from cloth. Mother bought a box (he having showed its worth on a dirty old kid glove) and haled down Bessie and Josie to see the creature. The exhibitor had a nice little set speech which he evidently knew off by heart and repeated like a machine. He said some sentences over several times for the benefit of each new beholder, till we learned some of them by heart too. "Lives on animal and human gore," "Eats, drinks, sleeps and lives head downwards, as you see," "Has twelve hooks on four different parts of the body," "Claws like an eagle, wings like a bird, fur like a mink, head like a black-and-tan dog — don't you think?" "Did any of you ever see a vampire before?" "I have seen many people in the course of my travels, but very few of them had ever seen a vampire," "It lives on beef, liver and tropical fruits," etc. etc. etc. You see, we didn't take long to learn some of his little details when we had heard them a few times and by the time he repeated for the last time I was ready to laugh right out. I was very glad he came in though and so were all of us, and I cleaned my gloves with the soap and it worked splendidly. After he had gone, I escorted Father in town, and then I went to Baldwin's and got a cup and saucer like the one Josie got from Bessie on her birthday and which I was so unlucky as to break

the saucer when doing the dishes a few days ago. I never told her about getting it and she went all through lunch and never noticed the difference! I wound up with the dentist's to make an appointment. Afternoon went with Father over to the Gardens. I think that is really all for today — I should think it was enough! (Lovely fine day, warm.)

Wed. 18th. Went with Father in town. After leaving him at the office, I went to Mr. Small's and told him to come for my "Harper's Young People." Then I went to Mahon's and got a lot of patterns for Mother and tried on jackets for myself. Brought three home with me on approval, one of which I kept. Nettie came in to lunch. After lunch Frank saw the vampire man going into Buckley's and as Nettie was very anxious to view this curiosity we two went over. Nettie bought some sachet powder and fully satisfied herself with the sight of the vampire, the soap and hearing the little speeches. Evening ran over to Winnie's to take back a book. (Fine with cool high wind.)

Thurs. 19th. Morning spent two hours at the dentist's. Afternoon to the Gardens with Father. Evening wrote to Edith Rand. Things seem to point very strongly to my going to Boston!!!! That sentence was to finish the line. (Fairly fine and cool, rather windy.)

Fri. 20th. Sarah here. Sewed a good deal and after went to Camp Hill for houstonia, there and back through the Gardens. Evening tried on new white blouses and kept one!!!! (*Very* cold, dull, wore winter jacket.)[15]

Sat. 21st. Sarah here. Afternoon to the Gardens with Father and planted my nasturtium seeds. Got a letter from Monsieur John I. Legro, but alas! it closes the correspondence. Ted left for a few days holiday at Berwick. (Fairly fine, slightly warm.)

In the Gardens, Halifax, N.S.

Thurs. 19th Mrng. spent two hours at the dentist's. Aftn. to the Gardens with
Father. Evng. wrote to Edith Rand. Things seem to point very
strongly to my going to Boston !!! That sentence was to finish the line. (Fairy fine call not windy.)

Sun. 22nd. Went not out. (Very rainy and cold.)

Mon. 23rd. Had to go to the dentist's this morning but Mother would not let me go because of the weather. Millie and Winnie were in awhile. Bound "Harper's Young People" at home. Josie and Bessie saw Mrs. R. Jones's new baby. (Rainy weather.)

Tue. 24th. Queen's birthday. God save our glorious Queen — long live our noble Queen! Afternoon went down to the Park with Bessie. Didn't go very far into the woods. Got some houstonia, a few violets, some buds of trees and heard frogs singing. Cars were just cram-packed full. Streets full of people. After coming from the woods went over to Winnie's to take her an "Harper's Young People." Evening studied houstonia and wrote this diary and drew these. Sarah here. (Regular Queen's weather, fine and warm though with cool wind.)[16]

Wed. 25th. Morning in town to make another appointment with Dr. Delaney as I didn't go on Monday. Afternoon Gardens with Father. Ted came home to dinner having arrived this morning but gone right to the bank. Mrs. Rand arrived evening to stay over night and leave tomorrow for Sackville where she goes to come home with Edith. (Fine, warm.)

Thurs. 26th. Horrid time with the dentist. Afternoon Gardens with Father and in town to get more material for Sarah who was here again. Mrs. Rand left about 1:30 p.m. Sewed a good deal, read a little and did a little botany evening but haven't time for more. (Dull, showery, though fair at times.)

Fri. 27th. Afternoon to my surprise and pleasure Winnie came for me with her carriage and took me around the Park. Millie was with us and so the seat was pretty crowded and the railing is rather sharp to sit against, but I was so glad she seemed to care enough to come for me and I enjoyed the drive very much. Evening wrote to Jamie Rand. (Morning rainy, cleared, became fine. Evening it was as foggy as ever. Cool.)

Sat. 28th. Now this is Agassiz's birthday and I have planned for weeks to celebrate it by walking down to the Park, but alas I couldn't manage it. Bessie went in town with Mother and Father wanted to go to the Gardens so there it was. Afterwards I went over to Camp Hill and got some houstonia. (Morning rainy, cleared; fine, cool wind.)

Sun. 29th. Church morning (Mr. Bond); afternoon read "Self-culture" and went out with Papa; evening church (Mr. Moore), and then for a walk with Ted, Nettie, and Wallace. Mr. Jim and Lucy were here when we got in. (Mostly very fine and warm with one or two showers.)

Mon. 30th. Morning in town to the dentist's and got through! Nettie was in to lunch and stayed till the 6 o'clock bus passed, which she took. Busy with various things. Ted engaged our state-room in the *Halifax*. (Morning dull, showery, afternoon rainy.)[17]

Tue. 31st. Mother is so "forehanded" that we haven't been a bit rushed today, indeed it hardly seems to me possible that when things go on so quietly that tomorrow we will really be off. Morning I read hard on "Self-culture" so as to finish it before I go, as Ted will return it before we come back. Afternoon went in town with Bessie on some last commissions(?) comisions(?) commissions (hope I've spelt it right at last) and Millie coming in just as we were going out she went in town with us. When we came home Winnie was just coming to see me so we all sat and talked in the drawing-room awhile and then they took an affectionate farewell of me. Last little things to do and will wind up with a bath.

June

Wed. 1st. Father's birthday — 76. Well, a good deal happened this day in that it ushered in our list of adventures. We were up very early, 6 o'clock and arranged our belongings finally; had breakfast soon after 7:00, took our farewell of the family and got off about half past. The morning was very foggy, which was a great disappointment to me because I was so anxious to see how the harbour looked down by its mouth. Ted was the only one down to the wharf with us. We stood on the lower deck, is it? and waved our hands and handkerchiefs till we couldn't distinguish "Edderd's" [Ted's] cheering countenance from any other. Then we went to our stateroom and fixed ourselves to spend the day there. Mother lay on the sofa and I sat on the end but after awhile I got into my berth so Mother could have more room. I wasn't the least bit sea-sick all day or night though I had a few vague uncomfortable feelings before I got into bed. I am afraid I am writing this very disconnectedly because it seems now such a while ago. Mr. Moore and his two sons were on the wharf; one of them — Ted, I think? — went on the *Halifax* with us. When Mother and I started for our stateroom we missed our way and wandered in totally the wrong direction. We came across the Purser — such a nice little man — to whom Mother introduced herself as she had heard about him from his aunt, Mrs. Harte. His name is Cook, and he would be the cousin of Carrie Cook. The waiter showed us our stateroom and after some time Mr. Cook came to bring us the key to our door and he sat down and talked quite a while. I think he is very nice indeed. He doesn't look a bit older than Ted; in fact, there was something about him that reminded me very much of Ted. He came in again in the afternoon and took our names and tickets and knocked off our door handle by accident.

Well, we had a great variety of music all day long. By turns, we heard the voices of two babies, a piano *horribly* played, the fog-horn, the dinner-bell, the electric bells of different rooms and to crown all, we had a hideous concert just outside our door in the evening. One man played on a wretched banjo, while the other accompanied him on the piano, and made up by noise what he lacked in execution. They both went at it hot and heavy; indeed, it sounded very much as if the piano and banjo were fighting and trying to see which could drown the other, and sometimes they got so badly mixed up you couldn't tell which side was beating. One man also sang three rowdy songs, driving me to the extremity of covering up my ears, though from the vigorous applause outside there were some who evidently appreciated the efforts. They subsided after 10 o'clock however, and at 11 the electric light went out.

The water all day had been very smooth, owing to the fog, perhaps, but it got much rougher during the night; still I slept pretty well and wasn't sick. Well, Mother slept pretty late in the morning (Thurs. morning) and I began to feel pretty badly, but I thought it was perhaps because it was so long since I had eaten anything. So when she woke I asked for a biscuit, took one mouthful, and — displaced it again. Well — (how many more "wells" for pity's sake) stirring about set Mother off and for the rest of the time she was pretty wretched. Mr. Cook came and said, "How are we now?" and we were obliged to confess to feeling not as well as we would wish. I was not ill very long though and soon felt much better. I felt able to get up, dress and eat something by the time dinner was being laid, and after a little I went up on deck. There it was

One man also sang three rowdy songs,
driving me to the extremity of covering up my ears, though from the
vigorous applause outside there were some who evidently appreciated
his efforts. They subsided after 10 o'clock however, and at 11 the
electric light went out. The water all day had been very smooth, owing
to the fog, perhaps, but it got much rougher during the night. Still
I slept pretty well & wasn't sick.

charming. The sun was shining brightly and the breeze was most refreshing. Land had been sighted and people were coming up on deck. I stayed up there until we were at the mouth of Boston harbour, going down now and then to see how Mother was getting on; she was dressed but lying on the sofa. It was surprising how warm it grew up on deck as we neared the harbour. Mr. Moore came up spotted me sitting there and stood a long while talking to me. Mr. Cook came along, said he was glad to see one up there, and was off again, and I didn't see him again to speak to. When we were past two lighthouses I went down for Mother and stayed below the rest of the time, she sitting in the saloon while I stood just outside by the railing. We were a very long time getting in, for first a custom-house officer had to come on board and then we had to wait for a steamer to move away so we could get into the wharf. Uncle Joseph was there to meet us and we had a high old time getting through the Custom House. The moment I set my eyes on this little man standing by the steps I had two thoughts: the first, "There's a typical Yankee!" — the second, "I do believe that's Uncle Joe!" and as it proved. We squeezed ourselves into a cab and drove to the Boston and Albany Station, and phew, sir, the heat was most terrible! We got on the train for Newton, and here Minetta put in an appearance and rode home with us. Next, we four and *all* our baggage crammed into a cab, and finally arrived here, and were greeted affectionately. Such a *lovely* place this is! Words fail me to describe it. After dinner, I sat out a long time on the veranda, and tried to keep cool, almost an impossibili-ty. Everybody is very nice and very kind to me and I am having a perfectly rapturous time. (I said it was fine and bright and *very* hot, didn't I?).[18]

Fri. 3rd. Morning sat in the sitting room with the others and did some bead trimming. When Mother went to take her nap I sat in our room and wrote the preceding account of our doing since Wednesday morning. After lunch I came up here again and wrote a two-sheet epistle to Bess. This took me a good while, so it was quite late in the afternoon when Cousin Minetta asked me if I wouldn't like to go for a walk. Of course I was charmed, so she and I and Mr. Ashe — (a young man staying here) — took a delightful walk around Newton. Mr. Ashe is of a botanical turn of mind so we can talk on that subject anyway, though he is not of a very talkative turn of mind; I think probably he is shy. He is a tall thin youth, with hollow cheeks, very dark hair in a mass above his forehead and big dark eyes. I think after dinner we sat first awhile in the parlour and then in the sitting room. (Rather cooler, dull, with a heavy rain storm which cleared off by the afternoon.)

Sat. 4th. Soon after breakfast we prepared to go for a drive and got off before 9, I guess. We have breakfast so early here. I am sure I can't describe half how I enjoyed it but I think if there is such a thing on this mundane sphere as pure unalloyed happiness that I experienced it this morning. We drove through most glorious scenery, reminding me often of the Cornwallis Valley, though when one comes to analyze

BOSTON, Mass. Bird's Eye View of the Back Bay.

The moment I set my eyes on this little man standing on the steps I had two thoughts; the first: "There's a typical Yankee!" the second: "I do believe that's Uncle Joe!"

it the resemblance is perhaps not so much after all. We drove to Dedham, to see an old historical house. It certainly was a quaint and interesting old place but more interesting to me was a group of artists on the other side of the street, all sketching away for dear life, except one idle maiden in a red shawl who sat on the stone wall behind the others and looked over their work and kicked her heels against the wall. I can't describe the country we drove through, it's no use. I can only say it was enchanting. Yes, and I forgot to say that they showed me Brook Farm made famous by Hawthorne. Sometimes we drove through charming woods, with several new kinds of wild flowers unknown to me, and then again we would come into open country and when we once came within the neighbourhood of the Charles River we kept coming in sight of that crooked little waterway every little while. What a pretty river it is! They showed me the place where the water is taken from to supply Newton. We saw many beautiful sights all the way there and back again. Mr. Ashe pointed me out two orioles and the nest of one — he and I sat on the front seat and Cousin Bessie and Cousin Minetta on the back seat. We got home about half-past 12 or 1 I think. What happened in the afternoon? Oh yes, we came up stairs after dinner. I wrote a two-sheet letter to Millie so she and Winnie would both get their letters the same day. (A good deal cooler but very pleasant.)[19]

Sun. 5th. Morning after breakfast I sat on the veranda railing a long time with Mr. Ashe and talked botany and he showed me some of his books, Gray's manual, two beautiful books of grasses with splendid plates, and two very interesting volumes of an old botany book published in 1801, which were very funny. After that I got ready and went to Grace Church with Cousins Minetta and Edith. After, read and by-and-by Cousin Minetta took me out for a walk. We went down a glorious woodsy road and coming home she showed me the grounds belonging to Miss Mary Shannon and the zinc-protected tree, where in times gone by Theodore Parker was wont to sit in its shade and write his sermons. Cousin Minetta thought she would take me to see Miss Shannon's garden, as we went in and Miss Shannon was just coming out so showed us all over it and cut me a magnificent bouquet of dentzia, yellow lilies, columbines, iris and other flowers. The garden is the dearest old-fashioned place one could imagine, just like the picture only ten times lovelier, and Miss Shannon is a sweet picturesque old lady. We got home rather late because they had asked a girl to tea on my account and she has already arrived when we got back. She seemed a very nice girl; her name is Mary Prescott. We had tea on little tables in the drawing-room. After tea Edith showed us her book of English pictures, *very* interesting. Cousin Minetta and I walked home with Miss Prescott by glorious moonlight. (Warm and lovely.)[20]

Mon. 6th. Started early (morning) on an expedition to Waltham; Cousin Minetta and Bessie, Auntie, Mother, Mr. Ashe, and I formed the party. We went into the town where we took an electric car and had a delightful ride to Waltham. We rode as far as the cars went and then Cousin Minetta, Mr. Ashe and your humble servant prepared to ascend Prospect Hill, while the others waited for us below. The climb was not hard for, though rocky (and I had only my thin shoes on), the ascent was not steep. We stopped a little below the summit and looked at the view and then we went right up to the top, and the scenery there beggars my feeble description. Away on the horizon was Boston; with the dome of the State House gleaming against the sky. Behind, between the Hill and the City, stretched Boston's "vast backyard" and such a one! Towns and villages nestling among the vivid green foliage, and the Charles River winding in and out, appearing and disappearing in its crooked way to the sea. The view to the

other points of the compass was chiefly hilly and green with masses of woods. The breeze was sweet and fragrant and refreshing, as though blown straight from the gates of Heaven. We could scarcely have had a more charming morning for our trip, and the beautiful clouds over the blue sky only added a new beauty with their tender depths overhead and moving shadows on the valley below. I felt like Gypsy Brentyn when she took off her hat she hardly knew why. So did I, but whether it was to see better or feel the breeze more or what I'm sure I don't know. I wanted to stay and stay and stay, but of course we couldn't and had to tear ourselves reluctantly away. We found lots of periosnopigusses up there and on the way. Mr. Ashe had a portfolio with him in which he put his plants, and very kindly mine also. He was very kind in getting me things. We finally worked our way back to our starting place, feeling (I speak only for Kate Shannon here) *very* hot, sunburnt, dirty and ecstatically happy. At the car station much to our surprise we found the rest of our party for we thought they would have been tired and gone home long ago. We had to wait a good while for the car to start so we got into the car that was all ready to go and waited there till it started off. We got to the Waltham Watch Factory just as the operatives were coming home from lunch, and we stopped there while they went in, and certainly the sight was worth seeing. Such crowds of men and women continuously filing in through the two great doorways! Three thousand of them! Young, and old, and middle-aged, and lame; and on the whole a very nice respectable looking company. We got home not sorry to have a good lunch, and after lunch I wrote a letter to Frank while Mother wrote one to Bessie (we received one from the latter this morning), and then I went into the sitting room and found Mr. Ashe at work on his plants so I fell to it, *too*, and kept it up till Mary Prescott's mother came to call and Cousin Bessie thought I had better go down to see her, so I rather reluctantly was fain to leave my inter-

esting occupation. We continued after dinner, and Mr. Ashe got through with his work very kindly putting my flowers to press with his.

Evening read Marjorie Fleming. What a dear quaint little thing she was. (Morning gloriously fine, and very hot, afternoon hotter with thunderstorm, cleared and was fine again.)

Tue. 7th. We didn't do anything in particular this day. In the morning I went around the "Plantation" as Mr. Ashe and Cousin Bessie call the garden. Wrote up my diary and a letter to Frank, finished my bead trimming, read "Jackanapes," and copied some "Nonsense Botany." I guess that was all worth noting. (Fine, cooler, but delightful.)

Wed. 8th. Morning Went with Cousin Minetta into the town on an errand; went into a shop to enquire the price of celluloid, and coming home from town we went over Elliot Church (Orthodox) and Grace Church (Episcopal). They are very handsome buildings and complete with classrooms, *kitchens*, *pantries* etc.! Just as we got to the house Mrs. Prescott drove up and invited us all to come over and sit on her piazza. (I don't think I mentioned that she called on Mamma the other day). So about half-past 3 she sent her carriage for us and Cousin Bessie, Mother, Auntie and I piled in and drove off. Mary Prescott was at a circus with some friends so she was not there when we first arrived. We had 5 o'clock tea out on the piazza, and the ice-cream was the most delicious I ever tasted in all my life — it was made of real strawberries. There was one other guest besides ourselves, a Mrs. Brown. About five or ten minutes after 5, Mother and Auntie drove home and Cousin Bessie and I stayed a while longer. Mrs. Prescott read us "Aunt Randy" out of Mrs. Slosson's book "Seven Dreamers." Neither of the others had heard it before so I didn't let on that I had. Before we left, Mary came in

Beacon St. at the Sommerset Club, Boston, Mass.

so I saw her for a few minutes. The carriage took us home in great style in time for dinner, but we hadn't much appetite. Evening we read "Lady Jane" aloud by turns and I worked on "Nonsense Botany" when I wasn't reading aloud. (Morning fine warm with pleasant breeze, afternoon colder.)

Thurs. 9th. Morning and after lunch we finished "Lady Jane" aloud. Mr. Ashe was away all day on a visit to a friend in Cambridge I think and didn't come even on the late night train. Afternoon Cousin Mary and Cousin Lucy Davis *and* Cousin Fluffy Davis drove here to see us. I was so glad to have seen dear Cousin Mary; what a sweet old lady she is! Wrote to Josie but it was not finished before Cousin Mary came. (Raining, close, and muggy.) [21]

Fri. 10th. Began the day with an ill-turn and had to give up dressing and go back to bed. Got up some time between 10 and 11 and for the rest of the morning read Agassiz's life and talked to Cousin Bessie. Mr. Ashe and the key turned up together — oh, I don't think I mentioned yesterday that the key to the big desk was missing and the desk couldn't be opened at all. I was half afraid that I might have mislaid it as I have been writing at the desk. However, when Mr. Ashe appeared after lunch he searched his pockets and discovered the key. Mother and Auntie went to Methodist prayer-meeting in the evening. Read "Agassagassagassagassay," and talked somewhat. (Fine, much cooler.)

Sat. 11th. Went downtown with Cousin Edith; went to

the Library and hunted in the "St. Nicholas" for John G. Francis's pictures. Afternoon went with Cousin Edith and a young lady named Marion Holbrook; the latter escorted us to her residence of her parents where their grandchild was disporting himself — a fine healthy-looking child with large dark eyes, though not a regular beauty. Two other babies and some other children put in an appearance, so we had a Babies' Reception. It was too funny to hear the wee tots calling each other babee! —— babee! After we tore ourselves away we went downtown and went for a few minutes to the Library. Evening started letter to Bert. (Fine, warmer.)

Sun. 12th. Went with Mother morning to Methodist Church. Afternoon lounged in the hammock and read. Evening went with Mother and Auntie to Methodist again, it was children's day and they had some very pretty music and exercises. But I was melted, though windows and doors were open. (Fine and *very* hot, nearly as hot as the day we came.)

Mon. 13th. Quite early, morning, Cousin Bessie took me and Mr. Ashe on an expedition. We took the train to Auston or some such name and then we took an electric car into Boston, changed that car for another, and finally brought up at Franklin Park. Then we took a wagon affair and drove all around the Park. It is a pretty place, but it can't compare to *our* Park. It is so trimmed up in places looking more like the Gardens than the Park. We stopped at the end of the drive (naturally) and picnicked among some trees and had a very pleasant time.

FRANKLIN PARK — SKETCH FOR FOREST HILLS ENTRANCE.

A small girl who couldn't talk properly attached herself to us and going right up to Mr. Ashe settled herself contentedly on his knee! She was a cute little thing but somewhat dirty. We came home the same way we went and I don't think I ever was hotter than when I came home, though a nice breeze had kept us quite comfortable all the while we were out. (Fine, *awfully* hot.)

Tue. 14th. Well certainly this is the hottest day I ever experienced. The night was horrible, it was hard work to sleep. We spent the day in almost absolute idleness. I tried to read but gave it up in despair, though by a desperate effort I *did* manage to finish my letter to Bert, begun last Saturday. I left off every stitch of clothing not absolutely necessary, turned up my hair and lolled in the hammock. Late afternoon there came up a refreshing breeze and finally there was a big thunder and lightning storm. Mr. Ashe went off on a trip to Lancaster; don't think worth noting, however here it is.

Wed. 15th. Morning got a letter from Minnie and answered Winnie's. Afternoon I was on the piazza reading Agassiz and watching a gray squirrel running about near me, when up drove Mrs. Prescott in her lovely carriage and got out here. So up I got to meet her, thinking it the proper thing to do, and she said she came to take Cousin Bessie for a drive or words to that effect. She went upstairs to speak to her and the next thing I knew she had asked me too! Glad? Oh, no of course not. So we set forth in that *lovely* vehicle, Mrs. Prescott and Cousin Bessie inside and I on the seat with the driver. We had the most glorious drive. Mrs. Prescott made calls at widely separated places so in this way we saw many points of interest; Brookline, Jamaica Plains, the Charles River of *course*, the Chestnut Hill Reservoir, and beautiful views too numerous to mention. All round we had a perfectly lovely time. Evening showed Edith how to make paper boxes etc. (Beautifully fine, and oh joy! much cooler!)

Thur. 16th. This morning we spent in Boston — Mother, Cousins, Minetta and Edith and I. We took the train into the town and then horse-cars; our first stopping place I think was Hovey's where mother bought silk for blouses for Josie, Bessie, and me. Next, I think we went to Jordan and Marsh's where all the cravings of humans can be satisfied I should think — except one's appetite; I didn't see any refreshments. Here Mother got some Canadian money changed and got some little things, and going down in the "elevator" (for the first time in my experience) to the basement we bought in the paper book department the "Rudder Grangers Abroad." Then we went to a smaller store where Mother looked over some things and we got three ties, a white one for Winnie and also one for me like it, and a pale blue one for Millie. We also went in to Huyler's, where Cousin Minetta treated us to ice-cream soda and into Shrieve, Crump and Low's, to see the magnificent jewellery, oh! We saw a lot of Boston but I haven't time to write much about it. We had a fine time all together. Nothing particular happened besides. (Fine and not too hot.)

Fri. 17th. This was Bunker Hill Day and fire-crackers lifted up their voices on the torrid air. The morning I spent mostly in the hammock. Afternoon wrote to Millie and there was a huge thunderstorm. Evening wrote to Josie. (Morning fine, very hot. Afternoon much cooler with big thunderstorm.)

Sat. 18th. Mr. Ashe came home yesterday from his trip to Lancaster. Left for good this morning about 11. Before going he gave me the flowers he had pressed for me and a book of Maine plants. He has been *very* kind to me indeed, but he has also snubbed me, which somewhat mixes me in my opinion. Soon after he had gone, Mrs. Buckham and Miss Willard came and stayed to lunch. We talked, and had a fine lunch, and about 3:30 or perhaps earlier they left. Edith and I walked down to

Tremont Street Mall, BOSTON, Mass.

Many thanks for your kindness
card very pretty. Josephine A. Beening · 4 South St. Jamaica Plain Mass

2133

the station with them and then we got a bonnet pin for me and some stamps, and went to the Library and hunted up "Davy and the Goblin." (Much cooler.)

Sun. 19th. To church with Mother, Methodist, morning. Afternoon stayed out on the piazza had tea as usual in the parlour; and after Mother had gone with the others to Grace Church, Edith and I went to Miss Shannon's and Mrs. Prescott's to leave some tickets. (Dull with nice cool breeze.)

Mon. 20th. Spent morning and afternoon on the piazza reading: finished Agassiz and read through "At the Back of the North Wind." Evening Edith and I went down to the Library. Coming home a big dog jumped over a wall and ran into me and nearly upset me. (Warm south wind.)

Tue. 21st. Morning quite early Cousin Minetta, Cousin Bessie, and I started downtown for a morning's excursion to Cambridge. We took the horse-cars at the corner and had a pleasant ride, the nice breeze keeping us from being too hot. We went through Watertown into Cambridge. I saw as we passed Lowell's beautiful old place, "Elmwood," Longfellow's old home with the homes of his daughters beside it, and the Longfellow Park in front on the other side of the road; also the house where Ole Bull's wife lives, and I think that was all of the places we passed that interested me much, though they showed me where Governor Russell and other Russell relations live. Oh, I've forgotten Mount Auburn — how could I? Cambridge is a dear quaint old place and I enjoyed seeing it so much. We got out of the car

at Harvard Square, and went to inspect the university buildings, grounds, and gates. We went through one beautiful gate built by a graduate, and walking through the grounds came out of another, without going into the buildings. They are fine large piles, and the vines on the older ones are very lovely. We crossed the road and went into Memorial Hall, where the darkies were cleaning up for Class Day I suppose, which is to be on Friday. The Gymnasium and Physical Hall or whatever it's called are near Memorial Hall. Then we went to the Agassiz Museum!!!!! If we hadn't been tired when we started to go I don't know how we ever could have torn ourselves away from this place. As it was, we would only get a general idea of what it was like; to study its contents thoroughly one would need to go there for weeks regularly. What engrossed us much more than anything were the wonderful botanical models all made of glass. Not only the flowers are represented but also the various parts highly magnified; whole, in cross section, and traverse section. We hugged those cases up the room and back again, at least Cousin Bessie and I did; Cousin Minetta soon got through and sat down to wait for us. After that we took a glance at some of the other specimens: birds, butterflies, animals, skeletons, corals, shells, fishes etc. etc.; we really couldn't take everything in in the time we had.

Coming out again, the horse-car had not appeared and we didn't want to stand there and get all tired out standing so we took an electric and went to the end of the track in Arlington. A communicative old gentleman sat next to me and made himself very agreeable;

I saw as we passed, Lowell's beautiful old place, "Elmwood", Longfellow's old home, with the homes of his daughters beside it, and
the Longfellow Park in front on the other side of the road

he said he was the first man to go over one of the Railroads we passed over; and he was going to be 82 years old in 12 days. The country was exceedingly pretty and it was an exceedingly pretty ride. The old gentleman very kindly pointed out objects of interest to me, but when near the end of the ride I asked him what monument that was we came to (a soldier's monument), he seemed to think it quite time to find out where I was born. I only hope he knew where Halifax, Nova Scotia was when I told him. Having some minutes to wait before the car started back we three went into a little store and had ice-cream sodas all round, then we got back into the car and had a lovely ride back. At Harvard Square we went into a hot waiting room till the horse-car came and we saw all the interesting places over again going back. We finished off our trip by driving home in a cab and having ice-cream for dinner. Afternoon sat on the piazza and read, and went with Cousins Minetta and Edith to Mrs. Merrill's and scraped acquaintance with Miss Bateman, her sister, a sweet young girl to whom I took quite a fancy. Evening went with the same for a walk around Mount Ida and Newtonville Avenue, and then sat on the piazza till nearly 9. (Fine, hot, with nice breezes.)

Summer '92.
(Lear glasses)

Wed. 22nd. Morning spent out in the hammock with Edith and Miss Holbrook, had lemonade and crackers out there. Afternoon spent mostly on the piazza and about quarter-to 6 went with Edith to the Library. (Fine warm, not *too* hot.)

Thurs. 23rd. Off junketing again, with Mother and Auntie. This time we started about 10 a.m. and took the train to Boston and then the train to Brookline where we were going to spend the day with Cousin Mary. We walked from the station to the house, being met by Cousin Lucy and Fluffy. Mrs. Mary Webster and Mattie Shewell came to dinner too. We walked and looked at some photos and went out to inspect the gardens and Cousin Carrie also took me into the Blake's grounds to see them. Magnificent they are, and make one think of old English estates. Cousin Sarah was not at home. After a sumptuous dinner Mattie carried me off upstairs to show me a new way to do up my hair, and made a very successful coiffure. (I may as well put it down here as anywhere else, that I had at last turned up my hair. I didn't want to a bit but they all seemed to think it was high time I did, and then the weather got so hot that I was glad to get it off my neck in spite of myself. I wore it on the top of my head, but the new way Mattie showed me is to have the hair parted and waved back off the forehead and coiled at the back of the neck.) While I was up there Cousin Mary came upstairs and when I came out of the room nearly deprived me of breath and articulate speech by slipping a bill into my hand. Dear Cousin Mary! I only hope I appeared grateful enough, I was certainly overwhelmed; — I did not look then to see how much it was as she seemed to want me not to make any fuss over it, but it eventually proved to be *five dollars!* Rapture. We drove home in Cousin Mary's carriage, much to our pleasure, and we drove around the Charles River Reservoir and saw Evergreen Cemetery and we had a lovely time alto-

Fri. 2[?] — morning. went in town with Cousin M and E., but the latter left
us when we started for the Art Museum which was our first stopping
place. Here we stayed awhile and looked at things in rapt admiration
lingering longest over the Acropolis at Athens, a truly beautiful model

gether! (Dull showery, at times rained hard but we were not out when it rained hard.)

Fri. 24th. Morning went in town with Cousin Minetta and Edith, but the latter left us when we started for the Art Museum which was our first stopping place. Here we stayed a while and looked at things in rapt admiration lingering longest over the Acropolis at Athens, a truly beautiful model. The other objects which pleased me most were some beautiful statues, particularly the Venus of Milo and the Apollo Belvedere; an exquisite picture of "On the River Bank" and another of a river by moonlight; and some magnificent Japanese fabrics. "On the River Bank" represented some peasants walking along by the side of the river, and the light falling on the figures and over the landscape was wonderfully lovely. This picture was immense, and was hung opposite a very large doorway so that from the other room it appeared as though we were looking out of a window right upon the living scene. After leaving the Art Museum we went into Trinity Church where Bishop Brooks used to preach. Then we took a car and went on some shopping for Mother and Auntie, after finishing which Cousin Minetta conducted me into Soule's photo establishment where I gloomed over the pictures and indulged in two mounted photos for Bessie and Josie. After this having three-quarters of an hour before our train left we hunted in a book stall till we found "Swiss Family Robinson" for Frank. Still having a half hour, we went into a jeweller's where Cousin Minetta wanted to make a purchase and here I was tempted into buying some sweet wee silver pins for Millie and Winnie, and I was going to get one for myself too but Cousin Minetta said *she* would give it to me, which she very kindly did. After that we took a car to the station and still had a few minutes before the train left. Mrs. Prescott came out with us in the train and very kindly drove us home in her carriage which was there at the station to meet her. The afternoon I spent mostly on the piazza, and evening a lady named Merrit came and stayed all night. She is an artist and has painted a lot of the pictures in this house. (Morning dull, very cool and pleasant; afternoon fine; evening rainy.)

Sat. 25th. Morning Mother and I got letters from Nettie, Bessie, and Ted and Jim. We stayed indoors morning and I wrote up my diary and scurried ahead in "Following the Guidon." Miss Merrit left after dinner when Mother and I were dressing so we didn't see her to say goodbye. She is a very pleasant lady, full of fun of a dry sort and very entertaining. After she had gone Auntie and Edith were going to pay calls and as there was a vacant seat in the carriage they took me along. I enjoyed the drive most thoroughly. The coachman was a very nice young man and drove me all around to the neighbouring roads. The first place we stopped at was as Mrs. Elridges's on Forest Street so "Tim" drove me around where we had a beautiful view across the valley to Waltham. We got talking about Halifax somehow (I think he asked if I lived in Newton or something like that) and in speaking of it he called it a "village," but corrected that to "town"; I didn't think it worthwhile to mention it is a "city." On our way to the next stopping place it came on to rain; we also had to ford a pond in the road at the side of a sewer in course of construction. We just reached the house in time to pile into it and to get the horse into the stable, and the rain came down in torrents. So while we waited Mrs. Davis (the lady of the house) escorted us all over it, upstairs and down, it being a house they have just taken for the summer. After that it came out quite pleasant and while Auntie and Edith were in the next place Tim drove me around Crystal Lake and into Newton Cemetery. Crystal Lake he informed me was once called Baptist Pond and people used to be baptised there. We went into the dear little chapel in Newton Cemetery; one side opens directly on a small conservatory where a banana tree in fruit and

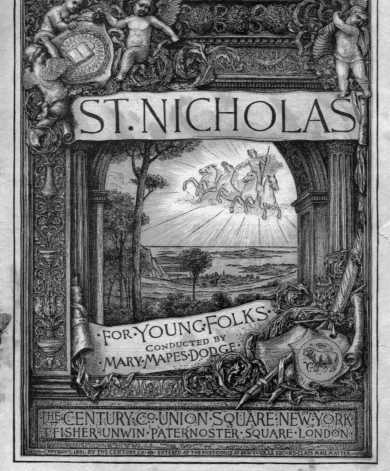

VOL. XVIII.   MARCH, 1891.   Nº 5

ST. NICHOLAS

FOR YOUNG FOLKS
CONDUCTED BY
MARY MAPES DODGE

THE CENTURY CO. UNION SQUARE NEW YORK
T. FISHER UNWIN PATERNOSTER SQUARE LONDON
COPYRIGHT 1891 BY THE CENTURY CO. ENTERED AT THE POST-OFFICE AT NEW YORK AS SECOND-CLASS MAIL MATTER

other tropical plants flourished. We had a pleasant drive home without more rain, but I think it rained again after we got in. (Cool, pleasant, rainy at times.)

Sun. 26th. Morning to Methodist Church with Mother. Mr. Bronson whom we like so much did not preach, but a brother whose discourse was on the crises in the History of the Coloured Race. His text was "Neither Jew nor Greek, bond nor free, male nor female" etc., and he said that there was contention in the North between the Jew and the Greek, in the South between the bond and the free, and all over the country between the male and the female. His sermon was good though flavoured with a good deal of "Our Country," and he closed his service with a remarkable scheme for raising money and a second collection was taken up there and then. The afternoon I spent mostly on the piazza and in the back parlour looking at photographs. Evening went with Mother, Auntie and Cousin Minetta to Grace Church to hear the singing which was truly magnificent. They sang "Tug of War Hymn" as a recessional; that is the hymn mentioned in the "Story of a Short Life" that Leonard was so fond of and they sang when he died. It was most inspiring. Dr. Shinn was not there, but a nervous young man preached. (Rather uncertain, has rained afternoon somewhat.)

Mon. 27th. Wrote a letter each to Ted and Bessie, morning. Sewed a little and finished "Following the Guidon." Afternoon Edith and I went to the Library and to Miss Holbrook for a short time. Evening went with Mother, Auntie, Cousin Minetta and Mrs. Doane to a piano recital by Mr. Carl Baermann in aid of an afflicted family. Oh what a treat it was! It was a great deal too short for me — I would have been delighted to have heard him begin and go all through the programme again. Two of the numbers were pieces Nettie used to play and sounded so sweetly familiar. Every single piece he played without notes, a most remark-

able thing. Had a lovely time. (Inclined to be dull and threatening rain.)

Tue. 28th. Why on earth didn't I write this day the next morning instead of leaving it till today — Thursday? Oh now I remember, I wrote to Jim and I think read or sewed the rest of the morning. Afternoon I stayed in with Cousin Bessie, all the others being out. Evening read "Davy and the Goblin" aloud. (I think the weather was doubtful but so am I too.)

Wed. 29th. Morning I finished "Davy" aloud and got dressed for company and started a letter to Nettie. Mrs. Davis, Cousin Mary and Cousin Lucy and Cousin Carrie came to lunch and Mrs. Webster came in unexpectedly afternoon. Some men at work in the chimneys very kindly(!) undertook to clean out a flue without warning, with a sooty result much to the chagrin of poor Auntie and the others. It seemed too bad when she was having company, but men will come just when and how it suits themselves no matter who else may be put out. Cousin Lucy gave me a dollar bill, it was so good of her. Now I have eight dollars and I have spent two or three already. Evening after a lively mouse hunt I finished my letter to Nettie and went to bed. Cousin Minetta left this afternoon for Harvard Hill. (Fairly fine, fairly hot.)

Thurs. 30th. Tried morning to study up something to write about in report which looms ahead of me but it was no go, the ground was too damp to camp out on and the mason's let fine gravel fall off the roof on me when I had settled by the back piazza. Don't know what I did afternoon, guess I read. Evening went for a delightful walk with Edith and Miss Barber — a young lady who came afternoon and stayed all night. They caught a firefly for me afterwards, which I watched when I was supposed to be going to bed. (Rather dull, afternoon rainy; evening pleasant.)

[Sun. 26th. Morning to ^Methodist church with Mother. Mr. Bronson whom we like so much did not preach but a brother whose discourse was on the crisis in the History of the Coloured Race. His text was "Neither Jew nor Greek bond nor free, male nor female." etc., and he said that there was utter contention in the North between the Jew and the Greek, in the South between the bond & the free, & all over the country between the male & the female. His sermon was good though

July

Fri. 1st. Morning read, sewed and had a bath. Oh I forgot, I also went downtown to post some letters and inquire after some gold paint which I couldn't get. Afternoon went with Edith and Miss Barber to see her off, and then we did a little shopping and then walked around and stood on a bridge over the railway and watched the trains coming and going. Evening Cousin Bessie and I concocted a composite letter to Cousin Minetta, great fun. (It rained at times, at others was merely dull.)

Sat. 2nd. Morning Auntie, Mother, Cousin Bessie and I went in town shopping. I don't think I care much to go shopping in Boston, it is much too confusing and too crowded, but I do like to go in to see something like the Art Museum, for instance. Stayed in afternoon until about 4:30 and then went downtown with Edith. Preparations for departure! (Beautifully fine, warm but not too hot.)

Sun. 3rd. Did not go to church all day and I don't think Mother did either as the weather was very uncertain, raining at times and hot besides. I read "Walden" almost all the time and also went for a walk with Edith, Sargeant Street around to Cotton Street and Newton Centre, and down Centre Street home. We had hardly got in when down came a drenching dousing rain, which I think lasted the rest of the evening but I am not sure. Got milkweed which I botanised next day.[22]

Mon. 4th Such a day! Firecrackers banged and boomed from one night to the next. I am glad we don't have Fourth of July in Halifax. Mother and I were pretty busy packing and afternoon I went for a most enchant-ed walk with Edith, down a glorious lane by Mrs. Francis's. We got into all sorts of beautiful woodsy, fieldsy, and flowery places. We got a lot of rudbeckia [coneflower], some scarlet lilies and a good deal of a kind of clover-like plant. We came back through Mrs. Francis's back premises, and I don't know when I've enjoyed a walk more. (Weather gloriously fine, not too hot.)

Tue. 5th. Tore ourselves away from our beloved abode in Newton and from Auntie and the others, and took up our wandering again on board of the *Halifax*. We had a glorious day. We couldn't have had a lovelier or a calmer one. We left Auntie's about 9:30 a.m. Mother and Cousin Bessie and the trunk etc. in a carriage and Edith and I walked to the station. At the Boston and Albany, Edith got us a carriage and bade us farewell; Cousin Bessie drove to the wharf with us where also Uncle Joseph joined us they both went on board with us and stayed some time, as we had got there very early, almost the first passengers I should think we were, and after they had gone and we had got out into the harbour Mother and I settled ourselves comfortably on deck with a shawl over our laps and enjoyed the scenery. We stayed there till evening (neither of us being sick, happily) and had our lunch and tea there. It was very comfortable on deck, more than when we went to Boston, there being an awning over our heads and plenty of moveable camp chairs. It was fun to watch the various people although we didn't have anyone we knew to talk to. Mother scraped acquaintance however with a very nice young married couple with a baby; the mother was pretty miserable and not very brisk and the father was *so* good to the child, which was only three or four months old. We were out

S.S. Halifax,
Halifax, N.S.

3509

Tue. 5th. Tore ourselves away from our beloved abode in Newton
and from dear Auntie & the others, and took up our
wandering again on board of the "Halifax." We had a glorious
day, we couldn't have had a lovlier or a calmer. We left
Auntie's at about 9.30 A.M.; Mother & Cousin B. and the trunk
etc. in a carriage & E. & I walked to the station.

of sight of land pretty soon as we were on the west side of the boat, you can see more from the other if you are coming from Boston; but it is the best side if you are coming in. There was a most glorious sunset, all blue and gold and purple and crimson and light and dark clouds, with the water reflecting the lights from all its dimples, and sailing vessels adding a new charm to the horizon against the glory. It was hard to go in and leave it but after seeing the best of it fade out we went below. I undressed and went to bed and had a beautiful sleep until nearly 11, when I woke up and ate some crackers. Then I went to sleep again and woke up about 7 and had more crackers. I really think that eating in this way keeps one from being sick, for I wasn't a bit sick the next day either.

Mother had neuralgia all night and was sick all the next day, till near the time we got to the harbour. I'd dressed somewhere about 9 or later perhaps and went up on deck where I amused myself by watching the shore (which was plainly visible when I came up) and my fellow passengers. The children were great fun the way they played together. The little girl asked the little boy where he was going, he said Nova Scotia, she said she was going to Halifax. Then they discussed which was the nicer place: the boy thought Nova Scotia was, the girl preferred Halifax. Another time a little girl left her chair for a few minutes and while she was gone a young man took it. She came back and did not seem very pleased to find it occupied but the young man happened to stand up for a minute and she promptly took possession of it and sat in it without his knowledge. Presently he went to sit down, first feeling for his chair and half going to sit down. Not finding it he looked around and it was too funny to see his face when he saw there was no chair there. It was lucky he didn't sit down flat on the hard deck. There was also a small boy who sat close to the railing waving a small yankee flag to the breeze, but he went to sleep with the little flag in his hand, a most pathetic little figure. He was the boy who was going to Nova Scotia, and his little sister was a dear little thing whose shoe-strings I was graciously allowed to tie up.

There were other children and all so sweet and good as they could be except one small boy who made terrible with the others, and a fat baby who cried when it couldn't have its own way. I never saw such a lot of kind, patient fathers together before.

I did not see much of the Brants (the young married people we took a fancy to) till Mother came on deck near the close of the afternoon. We were together then till we got to the wharf or nearly there. We saw Mr. Cook a few times but we didn't think he seemed as nice as before, he seemed to have got into a fast, smoky set which made us sorry about him for he is a fine young fellow and it would be *such* a pity if he went wrong, but a steamer is not exactly a helpful place for a young man. He seems to have a great tact with children, and told us about one time he took care of two babies for four or five days and nights; the passage was stormy and the mother was sick, so he took them into his own room and they kept him pretty busy feeding and looking after them. We got to the wharf early soon after 6. Ted and Frank were there to meet us. It was delightful to get home and see everybody again but still there is a sort of yearning for Newton within me. They don't,

Halifax, N. S.   by Moonlight

It was delightful to get home and
see everybody again, but still there is a sort of yearning
for Newton within me. They don't any of them seem to
like my hair up & it made me feel quite badly,

any of them, seem to like my hair up and it made me feel quite badly, though I knew they wouldn't. (Tuesday and Wednesday were as fine and warm as the heart could wish.)

Thurs. 7th. Nettie was in morning and stayed till 1. We got our things to rights pretty much. I think they all liked the things I brought them. Millie and Winnie came in for a few minutes before going to play tennis with Lalia Graham. I don't think they admire my hair up either. Afternoon I stayed in while the others were out and evening I took Winnie's tie and pin over to her and went in town with Frank, and when we came back Mr. and Mrs. Brant were here so we all entertained them and they stayed a long while. I think they are nicer than ever, but they are such sick looking people! Why is it that the Americans look so wretched? After the Brants had gone I started a letter to Cousin Bessie but I hadn't time to finish it before I went to bed. (Fine, warm.)

Fri. 8th. Morning finished my letter to Cousin Bessie. Josie went to the Gardens with Mrs. Brant. Stayed in afternoon. Nettie and Wallace were in for a short time. Evening down to take Millie her tie and pin and to the gardens with Frank, met the Brants. (Fine. Josie thought it was hot but I was cold!)

Sat. 9th. Morning in town to Reardon's to get bronze paint for mother to do the radiators over with. Helped prepare for a picnic which Josie and Ted got up to go to Cow Bay. They went about ten minutes past 2. Nettie chaperoned them. All went except me, I stayed home to help Mother; went over to the Gardens with Papa. I want to go to the picnic awfully but they thought there wouldn't be room for me in the van; but some people were not able to go and they thought they could take me, and I nearly went and then I thought I'd better stay. Evening went for a little walk by myself;

Gardens and got "potentella tridentata" by the edge of Camp Hill. (Morning hazy, cleared about 12; afternoon and evening fine. That was why they were so late getting off to the picnic, they were afraid it wouldn't be fine enough to go.)[23]

Sun. 10th. Rained, so I stayed in the house all day.

Mon. 11th. Sarah here. Millie came up to see me for a little while morning. Heard of poor Uncle Joseph's death, it gave us a dreadful shock. I wrote to Cousin Minetta in the morning after going for a little walk with Bessie. Gardens with Father afternoon. Nettie was in for awhile. (Fine, very hot, really Newtony.)

Tue. 12th. Sarah here. Wallace was in for a short time about lunchtime. Afternoon Gardens with Papa. Evening Mrs. Brant came up and after she had been here awhile she and Mother and Josie and I went and got ice-cream at Teas! (Like day before.)

Wed. 13th. Felt rather miserable (!) so didn't go out. Sarah here. (Fine, much cooler.)

Thurs. 14th. Sarah here. Mother got a pathetic letter from poor Cousin Bessie. They are all keeping up well. Mr. and Mrs. Brant came in afternoon. Mr. Brant has been in Pictou and P.E.I. Evening Mother went to help with refreshments at a Gardens Concert. (Weather fair, warm, a very slight thunder shower afternoon and another little sprinkle evening.) Got my Agassiz Association report off which I have been working up for nearly a week. Bessie took it off for me.

Fri. 15th. Stayed in all day; morning Josie, Bessie and I picked over wild strawberries for preserving while Mother took Nettie and the Brants for a drive. They went to Nettie's and Frank, who went too, remained there to stay with her for a day or so. Afternoon sewed

Band Stand in Public Gardens.

Soldiers Fountain in Public Gardens, Halifax, N.S.

Halifax, N. S.

Montreal Import Co., Montreal. No 901.

Eng. escorted Mother
over to the Gardens where there was a concert & she was to
help with the W.C.T.U. refreshments per usual. Came home,
went to bed early. J. arrived in the middle of the night. (Fine fairly warm)

and read a little and evening I went down to say good-bye to Millie who plans to go tomorrow with a party of eight other girls down to Cow Bay for a week. She wasn't in so I stayed awhile with Miss Willis and then came home and wrote to Cousin Bessie. (Cleared from fogginess, fine, warm day, evening fog coming in.)

Sat. 16th. Millie did go to Cow Bay this morning as we found out. Afternoon went to the door to see if she had gone. I finished my letter to Cousin Bessie morning; afternoon I planted some seeds in the garden — rather late! — and then about 6 o'clock Bessie and I went down to see Mrs. Brant. We wanted very much to see the baby but she was going to sleep and the Brant's were out so we didn't stay. I have not seen the dear little thing once since the day on the steamer and Bessie has never seen it at all, so we were greatly disappointed. Evening Mr. and Mrs. Brant came in for a farewell visit and sat quite awhile. They leave on Monday morning early. They are such nice people and seem so grateful for what we have done for them and pressed us to come and see them in Brooklyn. I am quite sorry they are going, it was nice to have them dropping in. (Mostly dull and foggy!)

Mon. 18th. Early morning went over to the Gardens by myself. The Brants were to leave about the same time but I did not see anything of them. Morning did dishes, practised, copied some "Nonsense Botany" in ink (I had done it in pencil before) and read "Télémaque" with Josie. Afternoon started to do some botany, didn't get very far as I went over to the Gardens with Papa. Evening wrote to Bert to ask her and the Baby to come too when Len comes down. I wrote in place of Mother whose eye hurts her too much to write. (Very fine, cool.)

Tue. 19th. Labour Day. Watched the procession pass here morning and drew a few members of the multitude waiting about here; I mean to say there was a mul-titude of people in the streets but those I drew were waiting on the steps. Of the departments of the procession the ones we liked best were the carette and horse-car horses and the feather renovating wagon, consisting of a bed with two old men in it. Afternoon stayed in till about 5:30 and then went over to see Winnie. Evening escorted Mother over to the Gardens where there was a concert and she was to help with the W.C.T.U. refreshments per usual. Came home and went to bed early. Ted arrived in the middle of the night. (Fine, fairly warm.)[24]

Wed. 20th. Morning went with Mother over to the Gardens to clear up after last night's refreshment business. Interviewed the loon which I first saw Monday morning and tried to hunt up a gardener to carry away the ashes. Was sent from one to the other and none seemed willing to oblige us, and when I got back to the lodge two little boys were taking them off. Stayed in the rest of the day. (Morning dull, cool; afternoon had a thunder and rain storm.)

Thurs. 21st. Guess I did nothing particular in the morning. Afternoon Bessie and I walked out to Nettie's. We found her in, and stayed with her till about 5:30. Didn't see Frank as he was down at the Macdonald's. Brought home some meadowsweet and furnitary from their place. We were very late getting home; we had to wait for the car in which we came home a good while. Evening went to bed early. (Very fine, not too hot owing to cool breeze.)

Fri. 22nd. Afternoon went over to see Winnie but she had gone to Bedford for the day so I came back. Sarah was here. Evening Bessie and I went for a walk, through the Gardens and to the cemetery for Bessie to see the tulip-tree in blossom there. Out on to Robie Street, across Camp Hill (getting three-toothed cinquefoil) and home. (Fine, warmish.)

Sat. 23rd. Before breakfast went to the Gardens with Bessie. Stayed in till evening though I wanted to hear the band at the Gardens. Evening ran over to Winnie's. She was going out but I stayed a little while while she was getting ready. (Morning fair, after breakfast rainy; afternoon inconsistent.)

Sun. 24th. Fine and hot, but I had a cold, so didn't go out. Went to bed early. Nettie and Wallace came in after I had gone. Following night or more towards morning there was a terrific thunder storm with very bright lightning.

Mon. 25th. Afternoon went down to see Millie who came home Saturday. She was out so back I toddled. Afterwards she came in to see me, and stayed awhile. (Fine and *very* hot.)

Tue. 26th. Afternoon Millie came up. We went in town and then she amused herself by putting up my hair in different styles. Josie went out to Nettie's to dinner with L. Black and Mr. and Mrs. Oxley. (Morning rainy, with slight thunder. Afternoon fairly fair, fog came in again evening.)

Wed. 27th. Morning got up early, and so did the plumbers who were here about 7 o'clock. They are tearing all the plumbing in the bathroom to pieces, and think they will be at the job a whole fortnight. Got a letter, handkerchief, and some newspaper clippings, from Cousin Minetta, morning. Afternoon went to the Gardens with Father about 5 o'clock, posting two dollars to the St. John's Relief Fund. It made me feel so funny, I wanted to give something but it was so funny to send it to the Editor of the *Herald.* I signed myself R. F. Newton (meaning "Returned From Newton"). Now I have only about 50 cents left, let us hope I will get more in time to make a decent Christmas preparation. Evening went over to see Winnie for a little while. I am reading Longfellow, have read "Evangeline," "Tales of a Wayside Inn," and now I am at "Golden Legend." I love his poetry.[25]

Thurs. 28th. Afternoon Gardens with Father. Evening went to get berries on Camp Hill with Bessie. Then Winnie came in to say goodbye and after she had gone we picked over gooseberries for preserving. (Beautifully fine, cooler.)

Fri. 29th. Morning Nettie was in. She, Josie and Frank went off on a picnic with Mrs. Tupper. Walked down to the Court House with Father, but didn't go to meet him coming home as he didn't know what time he could leave. Result of having no one with him, he didn't see a broom in the sidewalk when he went to move aside for a perambulator and fell right down in the gutter. I saw him from the window but at first thought it was some young man. Two men helped him to the house — fortunately he was very near, and more happily still was not injured beyond a strained wrist, some bruises and scrapes and a severe shaking up. Just before dinner I went with Mother to take some things to her place in the Gardens, the rest of the afternoon I stayed with Papa in the dining room. Evening Bessie, Frank and I went for a walk, down to South Park Road, through the gates, down the left hand road to the old grassy road to the shore, home Pleasant Street. Came home and wrote diary. (Lovely as ever, but still cooler.)[26]

Sat. 30th. Morning worked on some flowers I brought home last night — diervialla and aralia. Afternoon continued and about 5 went over to see how Mother was getting on with her refreshment table. She didn't need me to help but she gave me an ice-cream and a piece of cake, for which I now suffer remorse. After tea Josie and I went over to the Gardens, she sketched and I loafed. It was charming over there. (Rainy morning, cleared and was fine afternoon.)

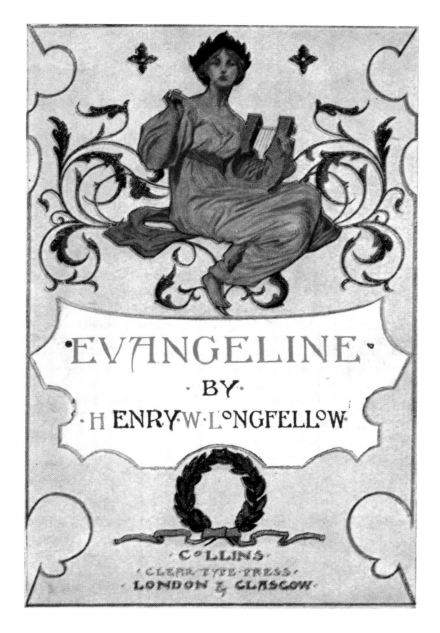

EVANGELINE

BY

HENRY W. LONGFELLOW

COLLINS
CLEAR TYPE PRESS
LONDON & GLASGOW

Long time over to see W for a little while. I am reading Longfellow have read Evangeline, "Tales of a Wayside Inn", & now am at Golden Legend. I love his poetry.

August

Mon. *1st*. Morning worked on some flowers. Nettie and Frank came in about lunch-time. Frank to stay at home now for good. He had a nice little change and looks much better for it. Nettie went off about 4 and took Bessie with her to stay awhile. After they went I went into the Library. Evening Frank and I went to a concert in the Gardens. The music was delightful, particularly "The Lost Chord," "Bohemian Girl," and the "Hunting Song." The latter has been played many times but I have never had a chance to hear it before. It was splendid. Mother was over there helping with refreshments. Saw Anna Mitchell and a young man — *and* Millie with a young man! What are the children coming too? (Dull, foggish, slightly rainy at times.) There were also very pretty fireworks over the pond in the Gardens.

Tue. *2nd*. Stayed in, did house work, read, worked on flowers etc. (Very rainy.)

Wed. *3rd*. Nothing at all wonderful or startling happened today. Got up early, had a sponge-bath and gymnastics, and was so busy with one thing and another that I hadn't time to practise. Plumbers here all day as usual, and working well into the evening. Started to go into the kitchen when they were all getting their tea — retired precipitately. (Weather is foggy and rainy as ever except for a little while in morning when there was a little misty sunshine.)

Thurs. *4th*., Fri. *5th*., Sat. *6th* and Sun. *7th*. Nothing very particular happened. Millie has not been up — don't expect her now, ever. Nettie and Bessie came in to lunch on 7th. Get up early, sponge, exercise and practise. After breakfast, routine much the same every day; usually going out with Father every afternoon if fine enough. Church morning Sunday. Afternoons went with Father to Gardens. Went to bed early. Guess that's

all. (Mostly dull, foggy, and inclined to rain except Sun. which was glorious.)

Mon. *8th*. Up early, Gardens with Frank, with sponge, exercise, and practise first. Afternoon same with Father. Evening finished training nasturtiums. Ted came home from Berwick. Now I'm off, goodnight — 8:45. (Glorious! cool breeze. Lovely!)

Tue. *9th*. Morning Gardens etc. After breakfast about 10:30 Frank and I went out to Nettie's, stayed to lunch; came home about 4:30, in the horse-cars as far as they go. (Early morning fine, cool; after dull, with cool high winds, with slight showers afternoon.)

Wed. *10th*. Didn't go to the Gardens morning, only practised morning before breakfast. Afternoon went with Nettie (who came in to lunch) downtown in the tram to help her carry some things to Wallace's office. Also went to Library, and got a block at Gladwin's — 15 cents. (Close, dull; afternoon fine.)[27]

Thurs. *11th*. Morning traipsed about on errands for Mother; preparations going on for Len and co. as we had a dispatch saying they expect to arrive on Saturday. Afternoon Gardens! with Papa. (Morning and evening dull; otherwise fine.)

Fri. *12th*. Morning Bessie came back from Nettie's. Helped generally and didn't go out. (More dull than I think.)

Sat. *13th*. Up at 6. Len, Bert and Baby arrived about 10. I think both look very well, and dear Baby is hardly a bit changed, I did not think there would be so little change in her. She trots all about, though, and talks in a funny little plaintive way. She has already caught Josie's and

my names — "Dozhie," "Tay-ie"! She is a darling. Poor Bessie quite ill with quinsey, had to have the doctor. (Rainy, rainy, rainy.)

Sun. 14th. To church morning. Nothing particular happened. (It was dull, fine, rainy and windy, mixed.) Nettie and Wallace were in afternoon.

Mon. 15th. Nothing particular happened, except that Millie for a wonder came up to see me and we amused "Beo" as the Baby calls herself while her "Mammy and Daddy" were out. (Not by any means settled, *very* rainy at times, warm.)

Tue. 16th. Len left early for Cape Breton. I expect, though not for certain, that Nettie and Wallace went off today on a driving tour through the province. They were to have gone first Saturday and then Monday but didn't on weather account. Didn't go out all day, but after dinner Frank and I went for a scanty walk South Park Street, South Street and Tower Road. I wanted to go for a *long walk* but Frank didn't feel inclined; I also very much wanted to go rowing with Ted, Josie and Bessie who went out on the Arm. I seem to be disappointed in almost everything I want now since I came home — except in Bert and Beo coming with Len. I'm glad I wasn't left there — no boating, no picnics, no drives, no friends to speak of, one being away and the other failing to connect pretty constantly. Still I can't say I'm unhappy, except when I'm in my own bad books and get morbid, and I think; when anything nice does happen I enjoy it thoroughly. About the worst of any of the above list of grievances is that I hardly am able to get a botanical specimen from one week's end to another, and what kind of report can I get up next month at that rate? Bessie is much better today her throat having broken yesterday. Afternoon I took care of Beo a good while while her Mother was out. Had her in the room where Bessie was so she could see her. She was just as good as

gold and perfectly fascinating. Enjoyed *her* anyway, if I *couldn't* go rowing! (Gloriously fine — at last!)

Wed. 17th. Don't think anything of importance happened. Probably went to the Gardens with Father afternoon(!), but I'm not sure. Have forgotten what I did. (Think it was fine though.)

Thurs. 18th. Now it may be that I have mixed up this day with Wednesday, and the events I am about to write down as belonging to this day should go to the day before. The fact is, I have neglected writing for some days, and more than that have got very mixed in my account of the days. Thus I was quite positive that yesterday (Friday; I am writing on Saturday) was Thursday and I never knew until I saw Father with the "Critic," in afternoon, and thought it funny it should come a day earlier than usual! Wednesday then, if my memory is not too mixed, I went in town with Father morning and then in again with Millie who came for me. Don't know what happened afternoon, but I think box from Newton with Uncle Joseph's watch for Ted in it came evening. (Very fine and warm.)[28]

Fri. 19th. Afternoon in town with Frank, and after we came home went to the Gardens with Father. Met Beo and Bert and Frank there. Didn't stay long in any place, too damp. (Dull, dampish.)

Sat. 20th. About 12 last night Len came back from Cape Breton. Didn't wait up to welcome him home though. Nothing particular happened afternoon. I and Josie took care of Beo while Len, Bert and Ted went to Bedford. Of *course* she was good — she always is with us! and *so* sweet, the darling! (Dull, damp, rainy at times.)

Sun. 21st. Church morning. Nothing particular happened besides. Don't know why I started to write today at all. Oh, I went for a little walk with Frank evening

when the others had gone to church. (Dull, damp, about sunset cleared.)

Mon. 22nd. In my mental mouth there is a marmalade taste — you know I don't like marmalade, there is too much bitter with the sweet. The whole day was gloriously fine with refreshing cool breeze just keeping it from being too hot. So Len who left early for P.E.I. got off in good weather and after he had gone Frank and I went over to the Gardens for a short time before breakfast. Nothing much happened till afternoon when Bert, Ted, Josie, Frank and Mother went out rowing as Mother wanted to call on Miss Lawson's on the Arm. They had a carriage (there go my glasses, off!) so Father went too for the drive and I went, too, to see him home safely. So after we left the others at Jubilee Wharf, Father and I had a very lovely drive around the Park. We enjoyed it very much and we could — here I had to leave off to go to bed and now I can't remember what "we could" do. But in the evening I said innocently that I would go to bed soon since there wasn't much fun sitting up, whereupon Father picked me up and we had quite an argument. He said he didn't like to hear girls talking so much about "fun," that I had a good home, parents, good health, etc. and that I should be contented with the gifts God had given me etc. So it has turned out I was discontented? Mother put a stop to our argument by the time I was on the verge of tears — why did I always get teary as soon as I begin to feel "emotiony"? — but I was sorry because I wanted to hear what next he was going to say. I felt pretty badly and went and read him some political things out of the "Gazette" instead of going to bed early as I meant to; whether this was to salve my own feelings or heap coals of fire on his head I don't know.

After Josie came up to bed I asked her opinion on the subject, and she was obliged to admit that she too has thought me discontented, whereupon my feelings again overcame me under the bedclothes. I am sure I *do* try to be contented, and I wonder how many girls of my age would be contented with the quiet life I lead, with the usual routine of dishes and going at a snail's space, so to speak, over to the Gardens? I don't say how many *ought* to be contented because of course all ought to be, but how many *would* be? I am sure I want to be contented and try to find enjoyment in everything I do, or, if that is impossible to try to do it cheerfully. I think I hate picking over fish more than anything else I do, but still I do that when Mother wants me to. Oh, no more of this stuff, I'm tired of trying to review my character and feelings. I don't think its healthy and only makes me morbid and unhappy. Let me do my very best to be a happy Christian, asking God's help — but I do wish someone would ever say anything to me about being a Christian! No one ever does; you might almost think they didn't care whether I was one or not! I sometimes think I ought to say something, but whatever should I *say*? and when? and how, without dissolving into tears? which in Cousin Edith we consider babyish, but what is one to do if one is built that way? — Evening Ted and Frank went to see some trained horses which were splendid.

Tue. 23rd. Morning went over to see Winnie who came home last night. Afternoon took whole care of Beo, her Mother and Josie and Bessie were out at an At Home. She is a darling. Took her to the Gardens. (Weather like yesterday.)

Wed. 24th. Afternoon took Beo to the Gardens for awhile and then went down to the Library. Miss [Josephine] Warren I think is now librarian, at any rate Miss [Mattie] Barnaby is her assistant. Glad old Cerebus is gone! (Like yesterday, perhaps cooler.)

Thurs. 25th. Josie and I went early to the Gardens before breakfast. Afternoon took Beo over to same place. Sat awhile with Miss Willis who was there alone. Had some crazy pains and felt funny. Oh, forgot to say that Nettie

Regatta, North-West Arm, Halifax, N.S.

Bert Ted Josie Frank & Mother went out rowing as Mother wanted to call on Miss Lawson's, on the Arm. They had a carriage (there go my glasses, off!) so Father went too for the drive & I went too to see him home safely. So after we left the other at Jubilee Wharf, Father & I had a lovely drive around the Park.

was in morning having returned from her driving tour. Went in town with her; she offered me ice-cream, but I heroically refused, oh no! What a thing it is to have a weak stomach!

Fri. 26th. Nothing much happened, except Winnie and Millie came in for awhile, saw the baby and were amused by her. Anything else? Don't think so, except I am much interested over "Children of Gideon." (Morning rainy. Afternoon fine.)

Sat. 27th. Morning about breakfast time Len put in an appearance. Nothing particular happened besides. Stayed in all day and had misery in my side. I do wonder if I *ever* will feel perfectly well, aboundingly healthy, for as much as a whole year at once? It seems to me as if no sooner do I feel well for a little while than I begin right away to get miserable again. If I don't have a cold and a nasty cough for weeks at a time, then I have cramps off and on, or a picnic some day or a night, or I get very nervous or something. Oh, dear, I hope that it is not dis-content. I haven't any wish to complain, I'm sure; I suppose if I was meant to have good health I would have it, *hein*? and I must be infinitely worse off. But the funny part is that I try to be so particular about what I eat, and when, and that; you might think that I should be well all the time. Still, who knows how much worse I might be if I wasn't careful? — Forgot to say Lucy Macdonald was here to dinner and afternoon. Evening Mother, Len, Bert, Ted, and Josie went to see the trained horses. (Dull and finely, hopelessly rainy and cold! Like September or October.)

Sun. 28th. Loafed indoors all day. (Weather too cold and damp for me to go out.)

Mon. 29th. Nothing particular happened. Bert, Len, Josie and Ted dined at Lucy Macdonald's. Nettie came in to lunch. (Rather dullish.)

Tue. 30th. Afternoon Bessie and I took Beo in the cars to Harris's to get roses for Mrs. Rand. It was rather fun, but Bee was very restless and inclined to be fretful so we hadn't quite as good a time as we thought we would. Same four dined at Nettie's. Poor Bessie, gets left a good deal. Couldn't *I* have managed the baby? Though five out of *one* family *is* a good number to have. I really don't think I am contented tonight, but we'll put it down in all charity to my having one of my sickly scrappy throats. Besides I get so ashamed of Halifax with its dirty sidewalks, disreputable Museum and forlorn Library, to say nothing of other causes of it disgust. And then I am so fearfully behindhand with my botany work! It wouldn't matter so much if it wasn't for the report stalk-ing ahead of me, and I thought I would have so much to say this time. Now I've relieved my feelings; will shut up and go to bed in a few minutes. Five minutes to 8 p.m. (Gloriously fine, oh, most delightful! warm too.)

Wed. 31st. So the last day of the month takes its depar-ture and with it Len, Bert, the Baby and our Edd'ard [Ted] who goes to spend his holidays, partly with Len, partly with Jim. Nothing much happened beside this noteworthy event. Millie came up this morning and stayed a while. Nettie came in at lunch time, was at dinner too and went up to the station. We had dinner very early — 5:30. The party got off just about 7. Father, Frank and I were the only ones who didn't go to the station. How lonely we will be! Especially will we miss the darling Beo. How can I ever write of all her winsome ways and baby charms? She is certainly the sweetest little child I ever saw — and so intelligent taking in everything and reciprocating! And such a dainty, lady-like little thing. Most children don't care how dirty or sticky they may be or how much they spill on them-selves and table, but Beo is a fastidious wee maiden. I might write all night about her and not get finished. (Weather rather muggy, morning; very damp if not rainy, but cleared was fine and warm for the most part).

Besides I get so ashamed of Halifax with its dirty sidewalks, disreputable Museum & forlorn Library, to say
nothing of other causes of disgust. And then I am so
fearfully behindhand with my botany work!

September

Thurs. 1st. Nettie came in and she and Mother went over to Dartmouth. Afternoon I went to the Library, and then for a walk with Josie out South Street, by the way of the lane. Evening Josie and I *took our first German lesson!* (Came out lovely, at first dull.)

Fri. 2nd. Did a little botany and French and German with Josie. Afternoon Gardens with Papa. Evening more German! Hope it'll do me some good! *Doubt if I'll ever learn much.* (Gloriously fine, but very cool.)

Sat. 3rd. Afternoon Josie, Frank and I went out in the Arrow with Mr. Rod Macdonald. We understood the message that we were to be at the Yacht Club at 2 o'clock, really it was 2:30 and the launch didn't put in an appearance till nearly 3! And we had all that time to wait! We had a very nice time; went down by MicMac Island, back, and up the Arm. Came home very hungry, for we got off in such a hurry. I had only time to eat a small piece of bread and a few mouthfuls of biscuit. Evening German (!). (Very fine, cool enough for September, but very pleasant.)

Sun. 4th. Had cold and didn't go to church. (Was fine and warm.)

Mon. 5th. Got up early to practise, but felt miserable and went back to bed. Nothing particular happened. Didn't go out I think but, being damp if not rainy, it is hardly to be wondered at.

Tue. 6th. Practised before breakfast, and spent the morning mostly in the drawing periopsnopigusses. Don't think I went out, again, but my memory is treacherous. I don't believe I ever said when the bathroom was fin-

ished. That was the first or second week after Len and Bert came. The passage was papered too. Then Mother had Maggie's room painted and now she has got the nursery ready to be papered — I'm sure it needs it badly enough. I have a new bedstead, the old one has gone into Maggie's room. What happened this day? Nothing particular happened. German, French and oh! *stewing* over a report, and reading "Katarine Regina." (Fairly fine sometimes, threatening rain and I think it did rain evening.)

Wed. 7th. Early practise, dishes, cutting beans, ironing, German and French — these filled the morning. Afternoon dressed, went to the Gardens with Papa and then did more German. Evening struggled a bit over my report — oh, what a wrestle it is! — had German with Bessie and Josie, wrote this and am going to bed. (Gloriously fine, cool.)

Thurs. 8th. Afternoon Bessie, Frank and I went to see the trained animals (horses), over in the exhibition building. They are wonderfully well trained and it is certainly most interesting to see them. The parts I liked the best were the Farce, the Drill (particularly the Oblique drill, when each horse put its head over the back of the other beside it) and the swing, but when they did some of the hardest things such as the rocking horse, the swing, and rolling cylinders I really felt sorry for the poor horses, they seemed to strain every muscle so. The man who exhibited them seemed very nice and kind although he did tap them with his whip, and he must have had wonderful patience in training them. — — Got off report, hurrah! (Gloriously fine, cool.)

Fri. 9th. Afternoon Lucy came in for Josie but, she having gone on a small picnic with the Payzants, I went

Provincial Exhibition Building, Halifax, N.S.

in town with Lucy. Went to various places and had ice-cream! (Finer than ever, warmer too.)

Sat. 10th. Really nothing particular happened, except Nettie and Wallace came in afternoon. Kate did not come with them — she and Mr. Jim are now staying with Nettie and Wallace. (Only pretty fair with one shower at least.)

Sun. 11th. To church morning. Read all afternoon. (Very fine out too cool for my silk blouse, which I wore.)

Mon. 12th. Up early and practise. Dishes, French and German, etc. Nettie came in after dinner and then Kate and Mr. Jim. At the same time I went for a walk down to the Park with Mrs. Tremaine. Was delighted to get to the woods again. Mrs. Tremaine is fun but she *would* humiliate me by talking to me about people whom I never heard of! I was glad to go with her partly because *she* wanted to go, but more, I am afraid, because I wanted to go so much I didn't much mind who went with me! Of course, I would rather have gone with Bessie or Josie, though the latter doesn't seem to appreciate my specimen hunting so much! (Just a perfectly perfect day, in every way! Warm as August.)

The Trinity Violet
Sept. 19.
a.L. Prat.

Tue. 13th. Nothing particular happened. Took a little walk by myself afternoon around and over Camp Hill. Studied plants, German, ironed etc. etc. besides. (Like yesterday, warm and glorious.)

Wed. 14th. Oh *dear* ! Nothing particular happened, but I *feel* horrible. Went over to the Gardens with Papa. Why do I feel horrible? What is the use of writing down disagreeable things? Only, Josie and I had a misunder-standing or something I don't know what you call it and she says I spoiled her breakfast and made her feel badly all day, which spoilt my tea and made me make an ass of myself in the evening. I may as well go on; it began by my getting up early, leaving my things to air, going down to practise and coming up again to call Josie and Bessie in good time and to put away my things. But alas my memory is frail, wherefore I sometimes have forgotten the last named duty, and Josie pathetically remarked that she wished I would try to keep the room looking tidy — that she had to put away some of my things every day. So I resolved she should not be able to say that anymore and put away my things when I went up to call her and now three flights of stairs is no joke, particularly when I always have to go up and escort Father downstairs besides. So, Mother was saying as I came down this morning that I shouldn't do it, it was too much for me. So then to give another reason besides calling the girls, I said that I went to put away my things besides, that Josie didn't like to have me leave them around for her to put away or something like that. Then, Mother must needs reproach Josie at breakfast, saying it was cruel to make me come up all the way up again, and it was a very little thing to hang up my nightgowns etc. I thought she started the subject herself — Mother I mean — but when Josie told me

International Yacht Race, Season 1905, Halifax, N. S.

that we were

We understood the message, to be at the Yacht Club at 2. o'clock, really it was 2.30. & the launch did n't put in an appearance till nearly three! and we had all that time to wait! We had a very nice time; went down by McNab's I. back, & up the Arm.

after I had come home with Father that I had made her feel so badly — she wouldn't have any French or German — she also said that I started it by saying that she didn't find any towels left around this morning. Now, am I to blame, or Josie? and, if I'm not to call her anymore — she won't hear of my doing it any longer, of course (and how she's going to get up in time passes my comprehension) — how shall I manage about putting away my things? For if I leave them out still I will only have to go up after breakfast which amounts to very much the same thing. This also brings up the question: ought I to give up my music altogether or keep it up? I cannot make up my mind on either side.

I'm sorry now I wrote all this down because it has taken so much space, and besides it isn't a very lovely thing to read over. Only, maybe, when I don't feel so very unhappy and *désolée (!)* over it, I may perhaps see where I was to blame, or what the trouble was. I wish I had a great deal of tact, and a much better memory. I went upstairs by myself after tea, to think. I felt badly and besides, I wanted to think about my music, what to do. Then Bessie must needs trot in and out — she's a dear girl, but once and a while she maddens me — asking me if I felt ill? Did my head feel badly? Did I know anything about her thimble? Was I going to bed? — (when I forsook the rocking chair for my bed). Did anything trouble me? I was cross and said I wouldn't tell her, and she said she should think I would be glad to confide in her, and I was contrary, and finally burst out that it was because Josie was cross with me, if she *must* know. Oh, we had a nice tidy little time and I feel pretty well ashamed of myself. I always do, you know, and I *will* cry when I don't want to, which I should think would be an interesting weakness for a doctor to study upon. For if I don't want to cry why do I? and Bessie said she must talk to Josie and I knew then the fat would be in the fire, and I bawled out for her not to dare to say a word about it, and Mother thought something was up, and

called up to know if she was wanted up there, and oh, there was a fine little hash. Then I heard Josie coming up, so I started down red eyes or no red eyes, and started to write this and oh - h - h, what a lot of room I have used up! Now what a pretty story this is to read! What a nice girl I am! (Nice and fair, warm.)

Thurs. 15th. Loafed indoors and felt miserable. (Dull, foggy, rainy.)

Fri. 16th. Last night we had no German and I went to bed very early. Got asleep before 9, I think, and the next thing I knew there was a great banging got mixed up with my dreams. At first, when struggling into consciousness, I was a little startled, but I immediately concluded it was Ted, for I heard a carriage drive off. I lay still a few seconds, thinking to hear someone go to the door but as no one went and the banging went on — though Frank was piping up below that it was Ted I heard no one stirring — so I ran my toes into my bed-slippers grabbed my wrapper and fled in pitchy darkness to the lower hall and fumbled for the keys. (It was a lucky thing the room was ready in time; it was papered and painted while Ted was away and Mother had barely got it in order and all). Before I got the first door open, however, Mother put in an appearance and drove me off the scene of action. I retired to the stairs and kept Frank company there. While Mother got the doors open and welcomed her prodigal son. Then we adjourned to the nursery — Ted's room I mean! — and got lit up, and there was a very fancy party gathered, I assure you — Mother, Bessie, Frank, and I all in various stages of wrappery, *déshabillé.* Poor Josie got woken up with the rumpus or slightly roused, rather, but she was too sleepy to come down; the furthest she could get was to sit up in her bed with her head toppling over her knees and send a feeble "hullo!" down to Ted. We did not expect our wanderer until tonight and the letter acquainting us of his departure didn't come till this

Quarry Pond,
Point Pleasant Park,
Halifax, N.S.

We went down the left hand road to the path by the sliding rock, explored about the woods, struck up through our old green picnic place, came to the path by with the rock in it, round by Quarry Pond, struck off into River R'd, thence to Inglis's St. & cars. Oh, the woods were lovely beyond description or imagination!

morning, which accounted for our surprise. Nothing particular happened today. Only I didn't feel very well but managed to toddle downtown with Bessie and came home in the cars around Inglis Street way. Have felt so well till the last three days! Why can't I keep so? (Came out *very* fine.)

Sat. 17th. Really didn't do anything in particular. Went to the Gardens with Papa afternoon. Began to read "Life of Mrs. Prentiss" and have got her married in the last chapter I read. (Fairly fine, cooler.)[29]

Mon. 19th. Felt rather miserable, rather blue, pretty nervous and cross and somewhat ashamed of myself thereat. Cramps are not good company. In spite of a rather bad night though I got myself up about half-past 6, in order to practise before breakfast. Nettie was in to lunch and was here a good part of the afternoon. Maydie Gray also was here awhile. What a bother it is to have all one's dresses let down, and what a bother they are when they are let down, all flopping around one's ankles! For my part I don't see why all the ladies don't wear their dresses only to their ankles, instead of either clutching wildly at their back drapery or collecting all the dust of the street with their trains! It is such a very sudden and odd change to have my hair up and long skirts that it gives me the very remarkable feeling as if I were playing charades all the time, dressed up for the occasion! That's enough trash for tonight. (Only so so, warm.)

Tue. 20th. Was up about an hour earlier than usual which is pretty early considering half-past 6 or so is "usual." The reason thereof was that Mother and Josie left early — 7 or so — in the Windsor and Annapolis Railway for Bridgetown; where they expect to be a few days also perhaps giving the Berwick folks a flying visit and the Rands a look in. They want to go by the Flying Bluenose but alas, she doesn't stop at Bridgetown so

they had to go the old old crawling road. Afternoon my new chum (!!!!!!) Mrs. Tremaine put in an appearance for me to go for a walk with her to the Park. So we went to the Point and interviewed the heather, came back Pleasant Street way and I treated Mrs. Tremaine to a ride in the car home, being pretty tired myself. Felt better today though or I wouldn't have gone. (Although there was a heavy storm last night today was gloriously fine though much cooler, or windy.)

Wed. 21st. Nothing very much happened. Afternoon I went down to Miss Willis's to take her some music; she and Millie were both out. Then I went for a walk by myself. Took an erratic course and came home through the Gardens. Evening ran over to Winnie's to see her and to take back some books; alas, she *woren't* in. (Gloriously fine, much warmer, warm as August I guess.)

Thurs. 22nd. Had a most glorious walk with Frank in the Park. Went and came in the cars which of itself was a considerable advantage. We went down the left-hand road to the path by the sliding rocks, explored about the woods, struck up through our old green picnic place, came to the path with the rock in it, round by Quarry Pond, struck off into Tower Road, hence to Inglis Street and cars. Oh the woods were lovely beyond description or imagination! I've found sarsparilla (not in bloom though), huckleberries, and lots of things. Brought home a bunch of sarsparilla, smilicna, pyrola and wild cherry blossom, star flower fruit, a teaberry plant in blossom, and some aster things. I also saw quite a number of linnaea blossoms which surprised me for I thought they were out of bloom long ago. Goldenrod in its prime, also the various kinds of "aster things." Saw *one* bluet blossom, and I think catillaire leaves, want to go again and get the blossoms when out. — Poor old Mr. Cronan died early this morning. He had had a long illness and a hard fight, but age told against him. (Perfectly raptur-

ous. Warm as a summer day, and with glorious gold sunlight of this season.)[30]

Fri. 23rd. Nettie, Lucy and Puss, Kate and Wallace were all in during the course of the afternoon for various lengths of time. Went for a walk by myself, Coburg Road, Oxford Street, Quinpool Road, across the commons from N.E. to S.W., and home through the Gardens. Morning worked on my plants from the Park, mostly, at evening wrote to Mother. (Weather not so fine, close and warm, atmosphere heavy, charged with odours of sorts, threatening rain.)

Sat. 24th. Morning more botany. Afternoon about 3 o'clock Mr. Cronan's funeral took place; it was a long one. Ted went, walked with Mr. Hagarty. After that I botanised more and read. Felt pretty blue and lonesome, thought of the girls and missed them dreadfully. Funny enough, by the time I settled down to read and forgot "dull, care," they both turned up and we went for a little while to hear the band at the Gardens. (Night and morning very rainy, held up rather afternoon with only slight showers; at sunset sky cleared.)

Mon. 26th. Nettie was in to lunch and stayed till 4 p.m. Did nothing much but read "Life of Mrs. Prentiss." I do wish I had known her, or that I knew someone like her, to whom I could speak freely everything in my heart. For if I am to be a good Christian surely I must say something to somebody soon, for ought I to join the Church? And there is not one solitary soul on this earth to whom I feel I can say anything of my own accord, without being asked. Oh, why doesn't somebody, anybody, speak to me? Do they none of them *care* whether I am a Church-member and a Christian or not? Or is the fault mine, and mine only? (Very dull or foggy, and rainy at times.)

Tue. 27th. Nothing particular happened. Got word from Mother saying they were coming today, so had a scramble to get ready for them. Mrs. Tremaine came for me but I thought I couldn't get off, and lo! after she had gone came a telegram to say they weren't coming till tomorrow. So I went for a walk by myself, Gardens, Jubilee Road, Robie Street, and across Camp Hill and home through the Gardens. (Gloriously refreshing, much cooler, very windy, fine and sunny though sometimes cloudy periods.)

Wed. 28th. Nettie and Wallace were in to lunch, and Nettie was here till about 5, when Wallace and Lucy came for her. After they had gone I went over to the Gardens with Papa. About 6 Mother and Josie got home; they had been to Bridgetown, Berwick, and Canard. (Most gloriously fine, warmer too, but wore a coat and found it none too hot.) Katie W. Shannon — Don't you think you'd feel better if that crack was plastered up?

Thurs. 29th. Was rather lazy. *Very cold* the greatest part of the day; about 3:30 went for a short brisk walk which warmed me nicely, then Josie started an ideal picture with me for a model. Result: a ghastly staring creature with a woody stare — but I think it will be good when she finishes it, as this is only the first sketch of it so you can't tell by that. I ground a crochet hook to get it to work better; filed it till it was the size I wanted. (Weather very peculiar. Morning very fine, much cooler and kept on getting colder; afternoon had some showers — morning too it rained. Now I come to think of it between showers it was fairly fine, windy.)

Fri. 30th. Nettie came in after lunch; Kate too was in to say good-bye — as she was to go for good in the evening — and Lucy and Josie went off together. Mrs. Tremaine put in an appearance after I had given up all idea of her coming and we had another walk to the Park, going and coming in the cars. Went up to Chain Rock this time. (Pretty fair, windy, rather cold, but warmer than yesterday.)

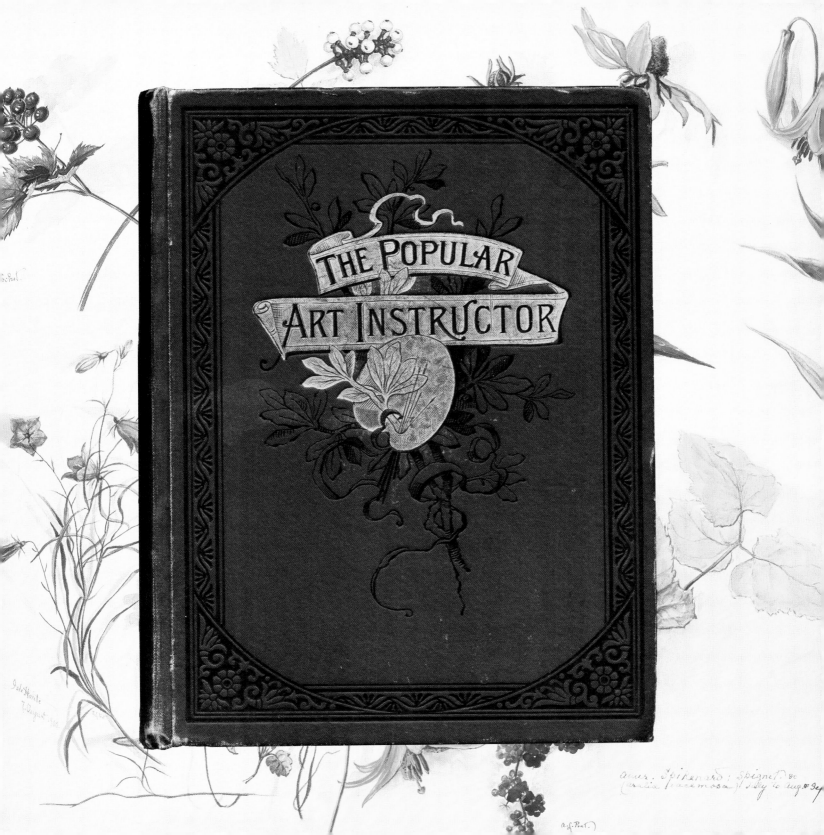

October

Sat. 1st. Morning Worked a little on some *nabalus* and Millie came up and I walked home with her. Afternoon went to the Gardens with Mother when she went over to the room there, came back and stayed in while Bessie and Josie were to see Frau Doering about music lessons for the latter, and when they came back Bessie and I went over to hear the band — this is the last concert — and waited and came home with Mother. Phew, but the wind was cold! (Only fairly fair; wind came up very cold.)[31]

Mon. 3rd. Morning started some lessons by way of a change. Josie and I have taken up "Telemacus" again and I *think* we shall have German after I've finished this. Nettie was in to lunch, she is about to move again into a house near the one she is in now. Poor girl! She'll be sick enough of moving if she lives out in the country and goes on the way she has begun and I'm sure she doesn't look forward to this excursion with unmitigated joy. Afternoon went for a walk by myself, Quinpool Road, Oxford Street, Jubilee Road, Gardens. Then to the Gardens with Father. (Cold as ever, fine.)

Wed. 5th. Very much the same as yesterday. Sat for Josie a good while morning; chopped tomatoes for chow chow. Afternoon studied. (Rainy; most terrific deluge downpour before lunch; afternoon sun came out.) Josie took her first music lesson from Frau Doering.

Thurs. 6th. Morning finished a letter to Cousin Bessie and while reading "Harper's Young People," broke the spring of my glasses, which made me feel pretty badly. Afternoon escorted Mother to a meeting at Coffee Room and took glasses to be mended. Frank's birthday, had some boys to tea. Nothing particular happened

besides; couldn't study, no glasses! (Fairly fine, evening rather rainy.)

Fri. 7th. Afternoon went to the Park with Mrs. Tremaine. It was perfectly lovely, a mellow afternoon with the sun rather obscured in a gentle haziness the air still calm, and sweet, with now and then a delightful breeze. The water, particularly in the Arm, was very smooth almost glassy, and the shore seemed very near and every object so distinct. The foliage has turned very much since our last walk, and is just beautiful, so rich and varied in all the shades of green and yellow and crimson and brown. We came around the Point and stopped at Chain Rock and went around past the Pine Hill and Bower establishments. Had a fine time found on my return that Millie and Winnie had been in so went over and saw *them* at Winnie's. (Fine, warm.) Bessie got my glasses for me in the afternoon so I am myself again.

Sat. 8th. Nothing particular happened. Sat most of the morning for Josie, also wiped off *all* the bannisters with a damp cloth. Dreadful, bothersome work. Afternoon in town with Bessie. Went to Library. In a bad temper tonight, going to bed. (Fair and really very warm, warmer than yesterday.)

Mon. 10th. Afternoon went with Nettie who was in to lunch. We had a carriage of course. Father, Mother and Bessie, out to Nettie's new house — I forgot to mention that they moved on Thursday and Ted was out there helping them. It is a very much nicer place where they are now — on the same road, but further away! Mother and Bessie went to pay calls at a couple of places on the way home as Father and I came home

alone having left Nettie at her house. (Fine, much colder N. wind.)

Tue. 11th. Routine pretty nearly the same as usual — early practise, study by myself — had no sitting today. Didn't go out. The halls are beginning to look *very* nice. (Dull, afternoon rained.) What *am* I going to give Millie for her birthday?

Wed. 12th. Afternoon walked by myself; took a devious course and came home via South Street. Josie and Bessie went to an At Home at the Payzants'. Nothing particular happened besides; I am nearly asleep now — five-past 8! (*Very* fine, cold brisk day.)

Thurs. 13th. Morning spent an hour and a half at Dr. Delaney's. Afternoon Millie came up (Winnie has a cousin staying with her!) and stayed awhile and I walked down home with her. (Fine, — *very!* cold and brisk.)

Fri. 14th. Morning went with Mother over to the Gardens while she cleared up at the "Lodge." Afternoon went for a walk by myself, round Common, over Camp Hill, home Morris Street Mother, Father and Bessie went up to Harris's for bulbs. Josie paired off with Lucy. (Fine, very warm — for October — mellow hazy day, pale golden ruddy and glorious.)

Sat. 15th. Afternoon Bessie and I went down to the Park; Shore Road, up past summer house, home through gates. Got brown and yellow sarsparilla leaves, and those bright red berries — holly I think. (Very much like yesterday.)

Mon. 17th. Nothing particular happened. Nettie was in to lunch. Afternoon went out with Papa. (Rather dull mostly, much cooler.)

Tue. 18th. Afternoon went up with Papa and Mama in the horse cars to see the *Blake* in the dry dock. We had a pretty good look at her but with Papa of course we couldn't go on board, or even to the edge of the dock. (Fine and cool.)[32]

Wed. 19th. Nothing particular happened. Afternoon went for a short walk, by myself, and pulled down my nasturtium vine and gathered the seeds when I came home. Nasty job. Going to bed now. (Dull, warm, damp, threatening rain.) Morning Got a letter from Cousin Minetta and a paper containing a verge pin for me.

Thurs. 20th. Morning went with Mother to Mr. Power's to take the key of the lodge and get earth for plants. Afternoon Millie came up and we went to W.C.T.U. with Mother and then sat in the drawing room. There was an eclipse of the sun today but none of us noticed when it took place though we thought the sun looked very funny. Ted and Frank both saw it though. (Cool, fair.)

Fri. 21st. Nettie came in but not to lunch. Morning in town and bought whisk. Afternoon Mrs. Tremaine came up and took me off to Belmont Woods and Maplewood. Home the same way and through Oaklands a little way. I never saw any woods so *glorious*, I think, as Belmont, the birches, oaks and maples were of such intense flaming colours, and even the witch hazels were showing golden. Belmont is far and away the loveliest of the three places *I* think. Had

The Acadian Recorder.
(Established 1813.)

SATURDAY, OCTOBER 15, 1892.

LADY JANE'S LETTER.

Girls of the Coming Generation.
AN AWFUL SOCIAL LIAR ABROAD.

The late Henry Pryor.—The Work
Exchange.— Mrs. Payzant's and
Mrs. Bauld's "At Homes."—Thurs-
day Night's Concert, etc.

The death of Mr. Hen___ ___
anoth__ brea__ ___

___ ___already many of
___ train of admirers, and are
accomplished coquette—a thing much to
···· ····

Mrs. Payzant had a monster "At Home"
on Wednesday, at which she forgot none of
her friends. The refreshments were quite
sufficient and grand enough for a large
evening party, and I am sure few dinners
were eaten by the guests that night.

a cold coming on, which was some drawback. (Fairly fine, very cold wind.)[33]

Sat. 22nd. Mother and Father went out to Nettie's to lunch. I was to go too, but had too bad a cold. Frank was out at the Webb's so there were only the four of us at dinner — *but* there were four of us. Worked on a whisk case for Millie most all the day, as well as I could for a horrid, weepy cold. (Fair, colder.)

Sun. 23rd. Stayed in and did nothing but lounge, eat, and encourage the growth of my first wisdom-tooth which appeared a few days ago. (Fine.)

Mon. 24th. Millie's birthday. Took her down her whisk and case. They really looked very pretty. The whisk was decorated with a blue satin handle and ribbon and bow; the case I made of white cardboard fastened up the side with blue ribbon and bows and a designed tracery in gold paint. Pale blue is *her* colour and matches her room. Afternoon she came up with some Recorder Puzzles which are on again, so we stayed in and worked them. (Dull and cold and not very pleasant.)[34]

Tue. 25th. Quite a busy day! No, is it possible that I haven't written in here since Monday! And what *has* happened since then? Don't think anything much happened; think Millie came for me to go in town with her but it was too damp for me with my cold, so she went without me. (Damp and disagreeable.)

Wed. 26th. Millie and Winnie came to see me afternoon. Nettie, and Lucy and Puss were all in too. Nothing else in particular happened; what shall I fill up this line with? um-m-m-m-m-m-m-m-m-m-m (not very pleasant, seems to me.)

Thurs. 27th. This was the busy day I started so bravely to describe on 25th. Mother asked company for next day, so all the morning I helped with various goings-on, such as beating eggs, frosting a pie for the first time! — dusting, etc. In the afternoon dressed and fixed my light stuff dress, went to the Gardens with Father, then did my hair in a *curly* way and dressed again. After helping with the dinner dishes I put finishing touches to my "twilight" and set off with Josie, Bessie, and Ted, to a concert in Orpheus Hall given by the Doering-Brauer Conservatory of Music. Josie sang in a chorus of girls, a lot of them; they made a very pretty sight. The concert was *lovely*, — oh, why isn't there another word to express it? Fraulein Budinger is perfectly lovely, so sweet and modest, with such a good figure and glorious voice! Herr Doering's cello solos were exquisite and were rapturously encored but he only responded once. There was a little girl played the cello too, and looked very picturesque, and did very well. There was a beautiful bouquet and a basket of flowers for the Prima Donna — though one was for the Frau and given to the wrong person by mistake much to the distress of the Frau's pupils, who had prepared it for her — and the Herr received a wreath of bay-leaves. We all wished he would put it on, but he didn't indulge us; anyway, it was so large it would probably have fallen around his neck! Josie wore a cream dress trimmed with narrow white fur and looked sweet. (Queer and showery, but not bad evening.)

Fri. 28th. Very busy, all sorts of things to be done. Nettie came in to lunch about half-past 1. Mrs. Breckan and little Paul came. It was good to see her again; she looks much older though, and no wonder — for she and the family have had a most terrible experience, their beautiful home being totally destroyed by fire. Little Paul is a dear bright little boy of about five or six, but he does not look at all like Egerton, and I don't think he could be called pretty. After a *very* good lunch — my frosted lemon pie was delicious — we sat in the drawing-room till Mrs. Wesley Smith came in

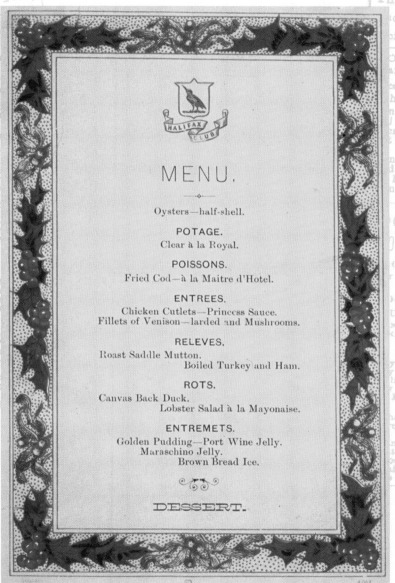

MENU.

Oysters—half-shell.

POTAGE.
Clear à la Royal.

POISSONS.
Fried Cod—à la Maitre d'Hotel.

ENTREES.
Chicken Cutlets—Princess Sauce.
Fillets of Venison—larded and Mushrooms.

RELEVES.
Roast Saddle Mutton.
Boiled Turkey and Ham.

ROTS.
Canvas Back Duck.
Lobster Salad à la Mayonaise.

ENTREMETS.
Golden Pudding—Port Wine Jelly.
Maraschino Jelly.
Brown Bread Ice.

DESSERT.

her carriage for Mrs. Breckan (who was staying with her) and took Mother for a drive too. I went down with Nettie to Wallace's office. Frank came too and Mr. Jim walked home with us two, but I feel very badly over that, for down in the Post Office he fooled me horribly and made me dreadfully mortified and mad enough to bite his head off — hope I didn't show it — and I don't think I like him much. (Began beautifully, dulled and began to sprinkle as we were on our way home.)

Sat. 29th. Dear, dear, *what* happened today? I think nothing much. Guess I went to the Gardens with Papa, and the weather was so-so?

Mon. 31st. Morning I *was* going with Mother in town, but Millie came up full of her puzzles, so, *naturlich*, I stayed home. Afternoon did nothing extraordinary, but went early to dress for Pussy's Halloween party. Shortly before 6 p.m. Josie, Frank, and I were all ready to go for the bus, when lo, Mr. Jim (ugh!) came in a hurry and whisked Josie off first for a drive and then out to his home. Frank and I tore down to catch the bus in such a race that I was perfectly weak when we reached our destination, and then we had to wait 10 or 15 minutes in the cold before the vehicle appeared and was ready to start. Then we were rattled and banged out to the Macdonald's, where Josie had arrived just ahead of us. The party was quite sizeable, mostly "kids" — Constance Bell and her little brother, Arthur Webb and his little brother, Arthur Payzant, who drove out — with Josie and Mr. Jim, Muriel Potts, Molly Robinson; such a pretty girl she has grown and so nice — and Nettie and Wallace, who came after dinner and Miss Altie Piers,

and we three. We played "I packed my bag," and "French Blind Man's Buff" and a splendid new game "Boots without Shoes" before dinner I think. I don't know whether you would call it "dinner" or not, anyway it was a delicious one, turkey and vegetables, rolls, cream pudding, charlotte ruse, snow pudding, fruit and candies, tea and coffee. After dinner almost everybody bobbed in a tub of water for apples and money. Lucy and Miss Altie also made a splendid little dwarf darky, with Miss Piers's feet and face blackened and Lucy [providing] the hands. She was a picture, and was perfectly splendid, so funny in her actions and so quick and witty in her replies and remarks, and kept us all in convulsions of laughter. We all laughed too a great deal over the "Morgan family" and over blowing out the candle blindfold; particularly when Mr. Jim tried it and Wallace turned him in the wrong direction and he turned himself right, and then Wallace took the candle away altogether and there he was reaching all over the table to feel the heat and finally discovered it had been removed. He is a funny goose, Mr. Jim is. He came in while Josie was writing anonymous letters to Frank and Arthur Webb, and then he must needs merely spoil it all by presenting Molly, Constance and me quite publicly with a letter each, such ridiculously silly stuff they were too; mine was "will you come and see the minister tonight?", no signature, and I rather think he wrote the same thing to each of us, such trash! I pitched mine into the fire when I got home which I did about 10:30; Mr. Jim drove Josie, Frank, young Payzant and me in. I had the back seat all to myself, didn't have to talk, and quite enjoyed the moonlight drive. Altogether we had a very good time, but I don't like Mr. Jim; I think he is a goose, in fact, queer. (Fine cool and brisk.)

THE PUZZLER

No. 388.—Diamonds.
1. A consonant. 2. A boat. 3. A local strike. 4. A country in Asia. 5. A fish. 6. To
1. A consonant. 2. An article of food. 3. An adhesive mixture. 4. A kind of hard bread. 5. A fruit. 6. An article of apparel. 7. A consonant.

No. 389.—Poetical Rebus.

Familiar verse from Charles Kingsley's Golden Days.

No. 390.—Transposition.

Transpose the following groups of letters to four words, of which the definitions in each case given. The initials of the words read downward will give the name of an easily tamed animal which we sometimes keep as a pet:

1. ACHDRRI—A boy's name.
2. RALPI—A month.
3. WECHIKR—A seaport in England.
4. TONEND—Something to wear.
5. LABALEIS—A girl's name.
6. GRELT—A wild animal.

No. 391.—Enigma.

No wings have I, yet I have sped to earth's remotest places,

A NEW FANGLED DANCE.

One Fuller Originated It, but Another Woman Copied It.

New York has a new dance and it has taken the town by storm. Loie Fuller, who has recently been involved in the air-ing in court of some very dirty domestic linen, was the originator of it, but she do-

We played "I packed my bag" and "French blindman's buff" and a splendid new game "Boots without shoes" before dinner I think.

November

Tue. 1st. In all day — Millie came up for short time afternoon. (Rainy.)

Wed. 2nd. Nettie came in after lunch and I went in town with her; went to Knight's and bought a copy of "Dominion Illustrated" and to Crowe's and got a crochet hook. (Raw, cold, dull.)

Thurs. 3rd. Stayed in — Millie came in for short time afternoon. (Rainy morning, damp and dull afternoon.)

Fri. 4th. Millie was up afternoon. Nothing particular happened besides I guess. (Weather bad I think.)

Sat. 5th. Went to Millie's to tea. Winnie, Lidy, and Lucy the only ones there. Played "Authors," writing games and "Literature." Had a good time and stayed late. Winnie and I came home together in rather rainy weather. (Dull, evening raining.)

Sun. 6th. To Church morning — Communion Sunday, which was torture to me and I was in a bad way all day. Since I do wish I was all settled and would stay like the rest. Mr. Jim came to tea. (Bitterly cold, windy.)

Mon. 7th. Josie and I went for a walk about 12 o'clock, Jubilee and Quinpool Road. Nettie came in to lunch. Then I went down to speak to Millie, and we went to the Library together, and she stayed here awhile. (Not very fine, colder.)

Tue. 8th. Rained pretty nearly all day, cleared towards evening and all but me and Mother and Father went to a concert in our Sunday School by the Coralline Mission Band. I worked very hard on a report and

finally got it all fixed up and finished but was very late getting to bed.

Wed. 9th. Spent the day out at Nettie's with Millie. We started from the home about 11:30, but it took us a *very* long time to get out there, because we had to wait so long for the transfer car to start. We didn't take long to walk the distance between the cars and the house, we walked as if for a wager. Nettie had almost given up expecting us, we were so late. We had a very good lunch, and afterwards talked in the dining-room, and left about half-past 4. We meant to take the cars back too but we felt so fresh we walked all the way. (Fair, fresh and cold.)

Thurs. 10th. Thanksgiving Day. Frank had Arthur Webb to stay for dinner and spent the day. Didn't go out; almost too dark to do anything, stupid. Frank went off to Berwick of course. Left yesterday. (Very rainy and stormy, snowed too at first.)

Fri. 11th. Winnie and Millie came in for short time afternoon. Stayed in with Papa while Mother was at a meeting and the girls were getting ready to go to tea at Mrs. Gray's. Frank came home evening delayed by storm last night from coming before. (Rather dull and I believe very cold.)

Sat. 12th. Nettie in morning. Went in town with her. Millie came up afternoon, sat in drawing room. (Lovely crisp day.)

Mon. 14th. Morning when I was doing the dishes, Wallace came in and said Emma had had to leave because of being so ill, and Nettie wanted me to go out

Market Day, Dartmouth, N.S.

and stay with her. So I got ready, and Mr. Jim's carriage came for me and William drove me out. Wallace taught me Halma in the evening. Ted and Mr. Irvine came up so maybe it was 16th. (Dull, cool.)[35]

Tue. 15th. Very busy all day. Had two callers afternoon. Mr. and Mrs. Richardson came to dinner. They are going away for good, so we won't have any more of their eggs. Helped prepare, clear and entertain. Stayed till 10 so we were late getting to bed. (*Glorious, warm and mellow like a day in September, sunny, and fresh.*)

Wed. 16th. All very late, owing to fatigue from last night. Nothing particular happened. (*Very rainy, windy, stormy.*)

Thurs. 17th. Very much the same routine — dishes, table-setting, dusting etc. Afternoon Mrs. Brookfield and Miss Piers called. Lucy and Puss came up to ask us up there to dinner — oh, and in the morning Nettie and I went to the dressmakers, end of Coburg Road. Evening to the Chief's about 6:30. Went across the fields by lantern-light, great fun. Miss Kellogg and her brother were there. Just had dinner and talked after about "stamps." Said that he had found that two cent stamps had come down again to two cents, as he had had to buy one, so I said that that was good for poor folks, as it saved a cent every time. He can't seem to let that joke die a natural death — conceit? though he didn't stir it up that day (Wednesday) when he drove Wallace home and came in for a minute. (Very warm, clear and became fine.)

Fri. 18th. Nettie made butter today, nothing particular happened besides? (Drizzly and unpleasant.)

Sat. 19th. Getting ready for "visitors" — which arrived, about 3:30, in the shape of Mother, Frank, and Dr. Sutherland (who arrived at home on Thursday.) Dear man, he is lovelier than ever, it is a sort of benediction first to look at him. I drove home with them as Nettie had Wallace to help her till Monday. Evening got Dr. Sutherland to write in my confession book. (Funny day, some time clearing, some time rainy, mostly dull.)

Sun. 20th. Stayed home with Papa morning. Dr. Sutherland preached. Wanted to hear him. Afternoon Mother, Ted and I escorted Dr. Sutherland to Robie Street where he gave a fine address. Mr. Irvine came to tea, and he and Josie, Ted and the Dr. (who went to tea at Mr. Moore's) went up to Brunswick Street where he preached again. Then when they came back we stayed and talked again.

Mon. 21st. Spent morning mostly in getting ready to go back to Nettie's. Dr. Sutherland was at some meeting but was back awhile before dinner which we had early in the day, as he was going to tea at the Lathern's and Ted was to have a young man to tea. Afternoon Mother, Father, Dr. Sutherland and I went for a drive around the Park. When Papa pointed out the lover's walk, and said what it was called, the Dr. said to me "let's get out here." Came home and left Papa. Josie got in instead, I collected my baggage and we drove out to Nettie's. Bade farewell to the Dr. with very great regret; he is certainly the loveliest man I know. Evening Halma with Nettie, and then she and Wallace played, I think. (Dull and cold, morning. Rainy, but cleared up.)

Tue. 22nd. Same as usual, I guess, all day. After 6

Robie St. Methodist Church, Halifax NS

evening we went over the fields by lamplight to the Chief's where we had dinner. After dinner Mr. Jim (who by the way said never a word about stamps, and presented me with great ceremony with a wretched apple) took Nettie to the Orpheus concert, and Wallace and I stayed and played Halma with Puss and Lucy. We two got back before Nettie, whom Mr. Jim drove straight home, and had to wait till after 11 for her. (Cold with a snow flurry morning.)

Wed. 23rd. Nothing particular happened — much the same as usual. Mrs. Foster brought Nettie's dress home. Afternoon a most phenomenal agent came to the door with his square bag and when told the lady of the house was too busy to see him he smiled broadly and cheerfully remarked "alright — alright!" and went right off at once, — if ever anyone heard of an agent departing with such dispatch? Ted dropped in before dinner but didn't stay. Said Dr. Sutherland left this morning. (Cold with snow flurries.)

Thurs. 24th. Busy as usual. Puss came up afternoon and she beat me at a game of Halma. Evening finished first strip lace for Mrs. Bolster's apron — only Xmas gift I have underway at this late season! (Cold, fine.)

Fri. 25th. Morning Nettie made butter. Afternoon beat Puss three games of Halma. Walked to the end of the road with her when she went home. (Glorious, cold and clear.)

Sat. 26th. Nothing particular happened; Winnie came home to lunch. (Early morning very snowy then somewhat rainy, windy.)

Sun. 27th. Very late morning, breakfast at noon. Ted came out to dinner which we had about quarter-to 3. Chief came over afternoon and stayed awhile. We were by no means inclined for an early tea, so shortly before 8 we had a sort of pick-up affair, which was much more fun. We didn't go to church because Nettie was so very tired. We held a council of war as to what we should eat, for Wallace forgot to bring out any bread yesterday and there wasn't much of anything to be had. There was only a small piece of the last loaf left which Wallace said would be enough with some jam for him. There was a bit of apple cake which Nettie said was plenty for her, and two tea-rolls which I said were plenty for me. So we made Nettie sit still while we got the tea, which we ate promiscuous-like, without substituting the tea cloth for the cretonne one. Wallace went off after his jam and found some cold potatoes; inquired of Nettie if they were wanted or if he could have them. Nettie said yes, and asked if he wouldn't like them fried, whereat I volunteered to fry them. So he assented, and I cut them up, and he got the pan and the cooking butter which also was nearly exhausted (we finished it between us), and while I was getting the potatoes underway Wallace was seized with the brilliant idea to scramble some eggs, which he did in fine style when I had removed my *chef d'oeuvre*. So with milk for me, coffee for Nettie, and tea for Wallace, the crust, the pie, the rolls, the taters, and the eggs, we made quite an affair of our picnic tea and it was great fun — only it wasn't much like any Sunday I ever spent before! (Cold with snow flurries.)[36]

Mon. 28th. Morning Nettie and I took the wash up to Mrs. Chalton's; afternoon Puss came up and beat me at Halma. As for Xmas things, even Mrs. Bolster's apron isn't done yet. (Dull and rather raw.)

Tue. 29th. Morning Lucy was in a little while. Afternoon callers, first Mrs. McInnis then Mrs. Miller and Miss Stytoie, and last, very late Mrs. Geldert. (Fair, coldish.)

Wed. 30th. Nothing particular happened, much as usual. Sewed an apron. (Very rainy.)

...ul butter, 4 eggs, ½ cup-
...easpoonful cream tartar,
...or jelly cake, and when
...between the layers: ½
...corn starch, 1 egg, 1 tea-
...Let the milk come to a
...starch wet with a little
...gar together, take out a
...d gradually beat it into
...rest of the custard, and
...thick. When cool sea-
...n the layers.

How to Make All Kin...
RELIABLE SPON...
Beat three eggs 3 minutes, add...

cold water in
which is dis-
solved ½ tea-
spoonful soda;
lastly stir in 1

SPONGE CAKE.

teacupful flour and mix thoroughly. Bake in a moderate
oven.

December

Thurs. 1st. Butter — housework — apron (finished latter.) (Mostly damp and misty; fair for awhile afternoon.)

Fri. 2nd. Nettie and I went in town to Mother's to lunch. Afternoon Wallace drove Nettie around to pay calls, and I scuttled round, went down to see Millie who was out, got a bath, and was barely ready when they called for me and we drove out to the Chief's for dinner. Went home I think as usual by lamplight.

Sat. 3rd. Wallace came home to lunch and brought with him a basket from Mother's. We opened it with great glee in the kitchen and found therein a loaf of bread, cookies, grass cloth for my work, dark aprons for Nettie and me and a mysterious parcel which felt when I took it like nuts and candies. Wherefore behold, my astonishment when on opening it, it was nothing but a package of shingle nails. This mystified me greatly and amused me so much that I laughed myself sore all the evening when I thought of it so wrote to Mother to see if she knew anything about it, and to thank her for the things.[37]

Sun. 4th. Evening went over to the Chief's to tea, and crossing the fields we saw a very peculiar red light in the sky, high above the horizon. It spread and grew brighter and wavered, so we concluded it was northern lights, but a few days afterwards the paper said it was only the reflection of a large fire. Nettie and Wallace and Lucy drove into Church and I stayed with Puss; she told me all about Frank's little party the day before and how Mother played General Post and Nuts in May. (Cold, rather dull.)

Mon. 5th. Nettie and I went into town a little after 12, took horse and car to Duke Street, went to Wallace's office; he and we went to the W.C.T.U. Lunchroom. Mr. Jim joined us afterwards and we had a fine lunch of "baked haddict" (as it appeared on the menu), potatoes, rolls, bread and butter and cocoa and tea — rolls and cocoa I had. After that Nettie and I went shopping, and then out to Mother's. Nobody there could tell me anything about those nails, but between their suggestions and Nettie's admission I got at the truth of the matter. Wallace got them and put them in the basket as easier to carry; when he saw I thought they were for me, he thought he would keep up the joke but gave to understand the rights of the case so I determined I would fool him a bit and not let on I knew anything more about it so as far as I know he still thinks I don't know. Nettie and I went off in the cars again, but, oh! it was bitterly cold walking after we left them! Dr. Bennett picked us up about Walker's,

NORTHERN MESSENGER

DEVOTED TO TEMPERANCE, SCIENCE, EDUCATION, AND LITERATURE.

VOLUME XXVII., No. 26.   MONTREAL & NEW YORK, DECEMBER 23, 1892.   50 Cts. Per An. Post-Paid.

"Every day Mrs. Peary and her husband took long walks on snowshoes, and often indulged in a sledge ride drawn by a Newfoundland and an Eskimo dog."

which was a great help. (Cold and dull, tried to snow.)

Tue. 6th. Nettie's day, but no one came but Puss whom I beat at Halma, and Mrs. Oliver whom Mr. Jim drove out. Struggled over some Xmas work. (Fine, colder than ever.)

Wed. 7th. Guess Nettie made butter today and I walked up Mumford Road. (Dull, cold, high wind.)

Thurs. 8th. Got note from Emma saying she would come next Tuesday. (Morning lovely; afternoon with a wind.)

Fri. 9th. Wallace brought me home a lot of cards for me to select from to send to the Bolster's, and wouldn't let me pay for them! (Rainy.)

Sat. 10th. Went in town with Wallace morning in the tram. Nettie didn't come; finds it too tiring. Mother had just got news when I came in of Bert's new baby girl, born on the 7th. Wrote the general Xmas list and then went in town on a shopping bout directly after dinner. When I came home they thought it was too late for me to walk out alone, so Mother got a carriage and she and I and Josie went out to Nettie's, where they stayed a short time and then went off leaving me with Nettie again. (Fair, cool.)[38]

Sun. 11th. Read "Pilgrim's Progress" and helped Nettie. Afternoon went for walk to the Dutch Village Road with a playful little boy who came from no-one-knows-where and attached himself to me. Had a glorious walk, notwithstanding the very bad walking, sunset sky, snow on fields, and trees, — oh, it was lovely. Evening Nettie played on the piano. (Morning snowy; afternoon cleared and was fine.)

Mon. 12th. Distinguished myself directly after break-fast by racing nearly to St. Agnes's, yelling at the top of my voice after Wallace who had forgotten to take Nettie's letters to post. He heard me and looked back, but didn't think it could be I, and went on again and I thought I should have given up. However, I kept putting on, hat and coat awry, blue apron waving bannersome beside me, skirts wrapping themselves around my legs and nearly tripping me up, rubbered feet padding away over the frozen ground, gasping, red, and dishevelled — I guess I was something to see. Then some little boys going to school stopped Wallace for me when I pointed at him frantically as I ran; so I hope those letters got posted finally. The day though beautifully fine was very cold and frosty and I breathed so short that it took me about an hour and a half to get over the bad feeling in my chest. Nettie had a little girl to clean the kitchen. Though only twelve she did as well as a woman. Nettie and I had a nice long day and I got on well with sachets etc.

Tue. 13th. Cold, brisk day. Millie and Josie came out early after lunch and stayed a couple of hours. Mrs. Sedgewick was the only caller. Nothing particular happened besides I guess. Emma too ill to come back.

Wed. 14th. and Thurs. 15th. I don't remember very well but I think Nettie made butter Wednesday and Thursday it looked too threatening to go to town, and snowed hard during the night following.

Fri. 16th. Got through early and were ready to walk to town when Lucy came for us with the carriage and drove us all the way, me to Mother's, and Nettie to town. Then I went down to see Millie and came back to lunch, to which came Nettie and Lucy too. Afternoon in town with Millie, escorting Mother to the W.C.T.U. on our way. Then went shopping, got Halma for Wallace's birthday and one for Frank from Nettie. After shopping went over to see Winnie, Lidy

1893

July
23 To 1 Bbl Flour $4 40
"   " 3 3/4 Butter 20   75
"   " 4 C. Meal 2 1/2   10
"   " 1 Bot Syrup   30
24 " 1 Pk Potatoes   16
"   " 1/2 C Starch   5
"   " 1 qt Salt   3
28 " 8 C Sugar   40
"   " 1 Pk Pepper   7
"   " 4 C Meal   10
30 " 1 Pk Potatoes   16
Aug 4 " C Sugar   20
"   " 4 C Meal   10
"   " 1 Pk Potatoes   20
"   " 2 C Rice   10
11 " 4 Butter   21 84
"   Baking Powder   10
" 1 Bottle Lime Juice   25
"   Sugar   20
" 1 box Soap   7
8 57

there too as usual. Stayed home evening with Papa while others were out, and stayed all night of course. (Fairly fine, snow out of N.E.)

Sat. 17th. Morning puttered round, Xmas list etc. till after 1, when Bessie and I clipped into town and I did up the rest of my shopping. After dinner packed up and drove out to Nettie's with Father, Mother and Bessie. They left me and drove home with Josie and Frank who had gone out to Nettie's in the morning. (Fair, mildish.)

Sun. 18th. Went for a walk after-noon to Dutch Village Road; lovely with snow and all but bitter-ly cold. About 5 or so Lucy and Puss came over and we went back with them to tea. They drove to church and I stayed with Puss. (Fair, *very* cold.)

Mon. 19th. Mr. Jim came to dinner. (Threatening all day, finally snowed.)

Tue. 20th. Miss Fraser, Mrs. Cameron, and Miss McCall called, with Lucy to show them the way. Miss Fraser brought Nettie a very handsome but not very pretty cushion. Got Bessie's mats done. Now Nettie thinks I have nothing more to do, and her present not begun yet! (Came up very cold with some more snow.)

Wed. 21st. Nettie made butter. Afternoon for a walk, short way down the Dutch Village Road. Evening went

to bed early to work on Nettie's present unknown to her. (Coldest day yet!)

Thurs. 22nd. Colder still. Ted came out to dinner. Nettie so funny, keeps saying "why, you've nothing more to do!" or "you're all done your Xmas work aren't you?"

Fri. 23rd. Very cold, colder than ever, with bitter high winds. Nettie and I wanted to go in town but couldn't venture. (Not been so cold at Xmas for ever so many years.)

Sat. 24th. Though colder than ever, not far from zero. Nettie and I went into town, but as there was little wind we scarcely minded the intense cold. A nice clear day with snow on ground. Nettie went to Wallace's, but I went home having completed at last my lengthened stay at Nettie's. Worked hard on her present and made one for Wallace. Millie came up after-noon. Stayed up till 12 trying to get through with my things. Jamie Parker came very late, about 11; train belated.

Sunday 25th. Christmas Day. Another happy Christmas! We had no time for stockings after breakfast before church, so left them for afterwards. Mother, Ted, Frank, Jamie, and I went to church, Bessie having unfortunately a bad cold. After church I hustled to try to get my presents ready for the big basket, and we had the stockings, one for each of us hanging on the screen in the

[Sunday 25th Christmas Day. Another
happy Christmas! We had no time for stockings
after breakfast before church, so left them for
afterwards. Mother, T., ?, Jamie & I went
to church, B. having unfortunately a bad cold. After

dining-room. They were not quite such fun as they were last year, and I was almost in too much of a hurry to enjoy them; still, it was nice to have them and some fun. Mine wasn't very funny, an old holey thimble, a few hairpins in a box, and a string of beads being the chief items besides nuts etc.! Nettie and Wallace came in to dinner, had turkey and pies etc. After dinner we adjourned to the nursery where we had the Big Basket of ancient fame. Had great fun over the thing, but the greatest joke of all was my present to Wallace which was the source of much fun. He looked so cheerful when the parcel was handed him, and thanked me with such a cheerful duck of his head. Well, he took off the cover, and behold, a wall-paper covered box, an old soap box in fact "done up in a handsome shape." Taking off the cover, another wrapper was brought to view with the inscription, "Mr. Donoll with Miss Shannon's respects." Under this wrapper was a pink-tissue paper package labelled "fur John, wid Biddy's Bist Wushes fur a happi xmus." Then the tissue made its appearance, with a label inside: "Wallace MacDonald Esq., from the Hobogoga." Beneath, a bit of white tissue paper, and then the final inscription " *But!* Mr. MacDonald — !" And *then* beneath this, a shingle nail, with a bit of pink ribbon around its neck! and Wallace clapped the cover on again pretty quick and wrapped it all up again. Well it was too funny for anything to see him; over every label he said to Josie, who was in convulsions of laughter beside him, "now, I know what this means; you may not know but I know;" all of them being jokes between us, "Mr. Donoll," "John", and "Biddy," being names we had for each other, the "Hobogago" being his rendering of the "Nobagoga" about whom I

explained to him two or three times, and the last being a quotation from some curious people who called on Nettie one day, and prefaced their remarks by saying abruptly "but, Mrs. McDonald", or "but, Miss Shannon" — "but, Miss Shannon, do you wear creepers?" being a remark to me which tickled Wallace extremely. I think I paid Wallace up pretty well for his take-in, eh? Josie and Frank and Jamie went to Sunday School. Nettie and Wallace went home about 4. The rest of the day I spent in reading mostly, just like usual. (Fair, very cold, with bitter wind, snow though for sleighs.) See next page for lists of what I gave and received.

I gave:
   Father : inkstand and pen (with Bessie) — 25 cents
      Mother : cup and saucer — 50 cents or 45 cents
      Jim and Lily — toilet mats — 4 cents
   Lily jr. : sachet — no cents
   Nettie: wash stand cloth — 22 cents
   Wallace: a nail!
   Len and Bert : toilet mats — 4 cents
   Beo : sachet — no cents
   Bessie : bureau mats — 8 cents or 12 cents
Josie : book — 45 cents
Ted : slipper case — 4 cents
Frank : notebook — 20 cents
Maggie : perfume (with Josie) — 13 cents
Millie : book — 45 cents
Miss Willis : calendar — 15 cents
Winnie : music book opener — no cents
Mary G. : handkerchief — 12 cents
Mrs. Bolster : apron
George : calendar
Charlie : booklet
Mignon : card

A MERRY CHRISTMAS

Should auld acquaintance
be forgot?

and with cards for Lidy, little Mabel, the Rand girls, and I clubbed with the others in a Halma board for Jamie. A good many of these things put down at very low prices (which I put down as nearly as I can remember) would really have cost much more if the materials had not been given to me.

I received: from
Father : microscope
Mother : apron and one dollar
Jim, Lily : a letter rack
Nettie, Wallace : fine new diary
Bessie : book "Fireside and Camp Stories"
Josie : little bag
Ted : blank tablet
Frank : handkerchief
Maggie : cup and saucer
Bridget! : silk handkerchief
Millie : book — "Knight Errant"
Miss Willis : handkerchief
Winnie : gloves and basket of candy
Mary G. : reel holder
Mrs. Bolster : needle book
Una Gray : basket
The boys : small plaque
and cards from the Bolsters, the Rands, Lidy; and a booklet from Lucy Cady.

Mon. 26th. Millie came up afternoon saw my presents and played Halma. Frank had Harvey Stewart, C. Cliff and Archie Blanchard to tea. Had great fun. Evening played bean-bags, and Up Jenkins, etc. (Fine, very cold I think.)

Tue. 27th. Afternoon went to take a present of Bessie's to Mrs. Woodbury, and went for a walk across Camp Hill. (Glorious day, much milder, bright snow, bright sun and sleighs out galore.)

Wed. 28th. Parcel came from the Bolster's. (Mild, dull.)

Thurs. 29th. Afternoon went down to Millie's (who is laid up with a sore heel) taking a round-about way for the sake of the walk. Evening Mrs. Knickle and Mrs. Annand came in. Jamie and Ted were at Nettie's to dinner.

Fri. 30th. Nettie came in about 2 p.m. Her girl came a day or two ago, so now she can go about a bit. It is Frances, Emma's sister, Emma not well yet. Nettie and I went down to Miss Willis's after I had escorted Mother to the W.C.T.U. only Millie was in. Stayed after Nettie had gone and played Halma with Millie — brought down the board to amuse her. Then went for Mother and with her to Mrs. Frank Parker's, on W.C.T.U. business. Evening Bessie, Josie, Frank and Jamie went to some tableaux at the Deaf and Dumb School. (Very much like yesterday, perhaps slightly colder.)

Sat. 31st. Lucy and Puss were in morning and Josie, Frank, and Ted went out to their house to lunch, and spent the afternoon coasting — goodness how I would like to have one more good coast! Afternoon I went down to see Millie and took her two little mince pies. Then she went out with Lucy and Winnie and I came home; sewed, read "Lass o' Lowrie's," and played some very exciting games of Halma. Good night diary and goodbye, to old fellow for its the last time I'll make an entry in you this year, or any year for that matter. You did give out a little too soon in the matter of paper but I fixed that didn't I. Only it will be too bad if anyone gets hold of these loose sheets and reads them! Today received first number of next year's "Popular Science News," with a piece of mine in it, and the new Appellation for me of "An Agassiz Association Observer in Halifax." Well, I must be off, so long, ta-ta, day-day, etc. (Fine, colder I think.)

"Le roi et mort - vive le roi!"

KATE WINIFRED SHANNON,
daughter of Hon. Samuel L.
Shannon, Halifax, N.S.
Born 13 March, 1874
Died 8 March, 1895 of consumption

Endnotes

1. Jean Louis Agassiz: Swiss-American naturalist.
2. *Harper's Monthly* and *Harper's Young People* were popular women's magazines from Boston.
3. Prince Edward was eldest son of the Prince of Wales and Princess Alexandra. Cardinal Manning: British religious leader who promoted religious education in schools.
4. *Progress*: weekly paper from Lunenburg, N.S.
5. Grip or Grippe: influenza, or bad cold.
6. Samuel Creed: librarian of Citizens' Free Library. Kate refers to him as "Old Cerebus."
7. Federal bye-election saw return of Thomas E. Kenny and John F. Stairs, both Tories.
8. World's Fair was held in Chicago, 1893. From Dan even to Beer-sheba: Judges 25:1.
9. Vasculum: a botanist's tin collecting case; cylindrical with lid opening on side.
10. *Lady Jane*: romantic novel by Cecilia Jamison.
11. Up Jenkins: game involving two parties guessing who held an article under the table.
12. College: refers to Dalhousie College.
13. Quinsey: inflammation of the throat or tonsils.
14. Wedding: Sept. 8, 1891, Nettie to Wallace Macdonald.
15. Houstonia: pale lavender herb; also called bluets.
16. Queen Victoria turned 73.
17. S.S. *Halifax*: steamship with Canada, Atlantic and Plant Steamship Line.
18. Uncle Joseph Ballister was married to Minetta Fellowes, Mrs. Shannon's eldest sister.
19. Brook Farm: West Roxbury, Mass. A communal living experiment depicted by Nathaniel Hawthorne in *Blithedale Romance*.
20. Theodore Parker (1810-1860): New England Unitarian Minister and abolitionist leader.
21. Mary, Lucy and Sarah "Fluffy" Davis were the daughters of Robert Sharp Davis and Judge Shannon's first cousin, Mary Harriet Shannon.
22. *Walden: or Life in the Woods* by Henry Thoreau is about his experiment to prove one could live surviving by one's own hands in harmony with nature.
23. Cow Bay: about 4 miles southeast of Dartmouth.
24. In 1892 the federal government established the first Monday of September as a statutory holiday called Labour Day. Until then individual communities declared local Labour Days.
25. Relief Fund: raised following a fire in St. John's, Nfld. that destroyed a square mile area of the waterfront. *Herald*: Tory Halifax daily.
26. Mrs. Charles Tupper lived at "Armdale" estate, Northwest Arm, not far from Chief Justice James Macdonald's home, "Blinkbonnie."
27. A wooden block to hold and shape hat .
28. *Critic*: four-page non-partisan weekly promoting Maritime economic interests.
29. Elizabeth Prentiss: American author of *Stepping Heavenward*.
30. Daniel Cronan: a very wealthy merchant. Died at age 84.
31. Frau Doering: teacher at the Halifax Conservatory of Music.
32. *Blake*: flagship of the British fleet.
33. All three were large estates on the Northwest Arm.
34. Recorder Puzzles: various word-game and image puzzles that appeared in the *Acadian Recorder*.
35. Halma: game played on a checkered board.
36. Cretonne: unglazed cotton or linen cloth.
37. Grass cloth: course material made from grass.
38. Victorian women rarely discussed their sexuality. Nettie was pregnant and had a son in April 1893.

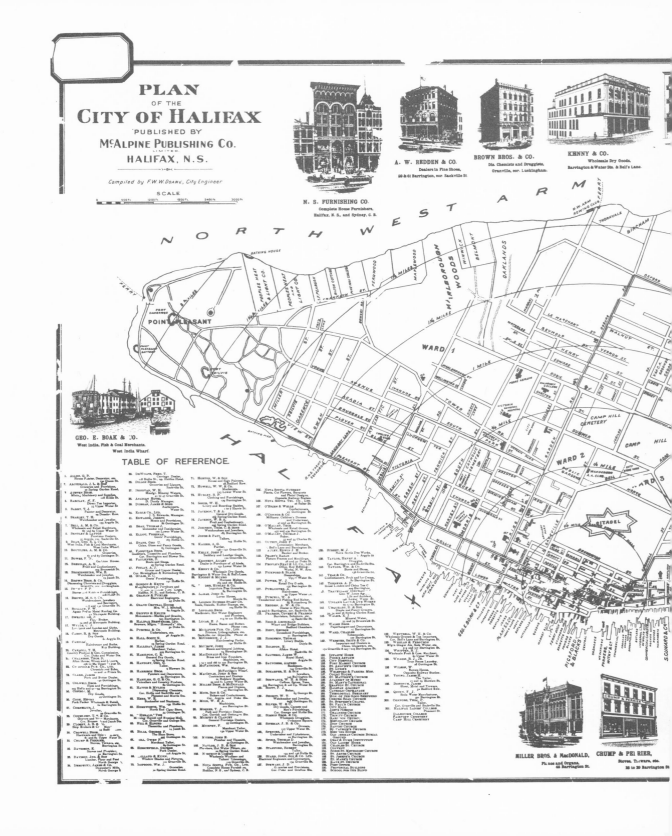